BLOOD HEART & SOUL

SUCCESS STORIES OF ENTRPRENEURS WHO MADE IT AGAINST ALL ODDS

PARMEET SINGH SOOD

PARMEET SINGH SOOD

STARDOM BOOKS

WORLDWIDE

www.StardomBooks.com

STARDOM BOOKS

A Division of Stardom Publishing

and infoYOGIS Technologies.

105-501 Silverside Road

Wilmington, DE 19809

Copyright © 2017 by Stardom Publishing.

All rights reserved, including right to reproduce this book or portions thereof in any form whatsoever.

FIRST EDITION APRIL 2017

Stardom Books

Blood Heart & Soul : Success Stories of Entrepreneurs Who Made It Against All Odds. /

Parmeet Singh Sood

p. cm.

1. Business / Self-help / Motivation I. Title

ISBN-13: 978-1545396445

ISBN-10: 1545396442

DEDICATION

To My Dad

DISCLAIMER

The views, opinions and information presented in this book are from the co-authors of the publication. The publisher does not endorse or subscribe to the information; reader discretion is solicited.

This book is designed to provide information on how each one of the co-authors did what they did, as their own personal narrative. It is sold with the understanding that neither the co-authors nor the publisher is engaged in rendering legal, accounting or other professional services. If legal or other professional advice is warranted, the services of an appropriate professional should be sought. Also, this book cannot be an exhaustive and complete presentation on the topics within the book. While every effort has been made to make the information presented here as complete and accurate as possible, it may contain errors, omissions or information that was accurate as of its publication but subsequently has become outdated by marketplace or industry changes or conditions, new laws or regulations, or other circumstances.

Neither the co-authors nor the publisher accepts any liability or responsibility to any person or entity with respect to any loss or damage alleged to have been caused, directly or indirectly, by the information, ideas, opinions or other content in this book. If you do not agree to these terms, you should immediately return this book for full refund.

FOREWORD

As a person I have constantly being on the journey of learning and have been updating my knowledge through reading a lot of books, attending a lot of seminars and above all having some great mentors in my life.

I have been the Eklayva, to many a Dronacharyas in my life and have learnt a lot by imbibing the practices and habits of successful people. If I Look back at my life, I have been inspired the most by people who have started from scratch and created a name for themselves in their respective fields, especially Entrepreneurs and that bias comes, as I am one of them as well.

The idea for writing a book like this came in my head during one discussion with a friend who was constantly in the belief that learning from the big heroic figures was one thing, however it was not possible to implement what they practiced as the size of the business that we operate are smaller and being an Indian Entrepreneur was a completely different piece of cake. I tried finding some material on stories of mid size entrepreneurs and could not find anything interesting or inspiring enough which someone could directly relate with one's own journey and take some lesson.

That's when I decided that why not I write a book about some such stories and try and bridge that gap in mindset of people who want to emulate from people they read about but get stopped as they feel that those stories cannot be related.

Each story is great and unique in its own self and personally provided me with a lot of learning and insight for my own business as well as personal growth. I hope that this book will go a long way in enhancing the lives of all the people who read through the pages and chapters and imbibe common traits/habits/practices coming about in each of these stories.

The secret bridge between thought and result is action. I hope that this book plants a lot of seeds of thought and you take action from the learning in these stories to your life and create awesome growth in your respective fields.

It really takes Blood, Heart and Soul to live the life of your dreams and these stories depict just that.

All the best!

Parmeet Singh Sood

CONTENTS

#	Title	Author	Page
1	ARE YOU DOING THINGS RIGHT OR DOING THE RIGHT THINGS?	BY PARMEET SINGH	1
2	THE ROAD LESS TRAVELED	BY RAJESH DEMBLA	15
3	UNBRIDLED IMAGINATION	BY THUMBAY MOIDEEN	35
4	EMBRACE CHANGE	BY ROHIT BAGARIA	47
5	WHERE KNOWLEDGE FAILS, FAITH TRIUMPHS	BY DR. MONIKA SINGH	63
6	THE RISE OF THE PHOENIX	BY SADANANDA MURTHY	81
7	CRAFTING DREAMS	BY BHAKTI SANGHAVI	97
8	SUCCESS: A CHIMERA	BY AVINASH SISODE	111
9	WHAT KITE ARE YOU FLYING?	BY VIVEK AGARWAL	129
10	PURSUIT OF SUCCESS	BY DR. SUNIL KUMAR	141
11	CHANGE FOR HAPPINESS	BY ASHOK SOOTA	153

PARMEET SINGH SOOD

ACKNOWLEDGMENTS

I like to personally thank each of these great entrepreneurs whom I met on the journey to write this book and they were gracious enough to share their stories on how they created success through the hardships and all ups and downs on the way. Thank You so much for your time and more importantly sharing from your heart.

I thank my beautiful wife Aveen Kaur Sood for giving me the space, time and motivation for me to take this plunge of being an author, which demands a lot of time, energy and dedicated effort.

I would also like to thank my dear friend Rajiv Talreja who inspired me to take on this challenge inside of my busy routine and its because of him I got the experience and made friends with all these beautiful people who's stories are published in my book. Rajiv is himself a celebrated speaker and trainer and the author of international bestseller book "Lead or Bleed."

1

ARE YOU DOING THINGS RIGHT OR DOING THE RIGHT THINGS?

- BY PARMEET SINGH SOOD, ENTREPRENEUR, AUTHOR, SPEAKER, TRAINER

A leader is one who sees more than others see, who sees farther than others see and who sees before others see.

These words by author Leroy Eimes have been my guiding principle.

There's a sea of difference in doing things right vs. doing the right things. Managers and management are for doing things right, whereas, leaders are focused on doing the right things.

I was able to transform Climax Overseas, an automotive rubber components exporting company, from a small scale industry with a 60-member workforce into a pioneering multi-million dollar business over a period of less than 15 years primarily because of one reason: my unflinching faith in myself. Even when my own kith and kin opposed my ambitions and propositions, I did not cower. I stood upright and trod the path I chalked out for myself with the conviction that if I succeeded it would be a vindication of my vision and foresight and if I failed it would only be a learning process.

In 1968, my father, Daljit Singh Sood started Climax Overseas with a lean investment of just Rs. 1,000. He acquired knowledge of rubber technology over the next one decade through extensive reading and research and went on to establish his name in the field of rubber technology at a time when there were very few such entrepreneurs in this industry, in the country.

Discovering Life's Calling

Although, right from the beginning, I have rebelled against my father's ideas of how to do business, I think, he has been my guide and mentor as far as finding an answer to why do business. After I discovered the *why* of business, the *how* of business fell in line with great clarity. He sowed the seeds of this angst and also helped me discover the answer.

In 1999, after my graduation, I wanted to pursue post-graduation in business management in the US and make a living in that country. I did not want to join the family business because, at that time, I thought it was not a white-collar business. In my youthful hotheadedness, I dreamed of being a part of something more glamorous; something bigger and better. My father didn't approve; he wanted me to join the family business.

We had a lot of arguments regarding this issue. One argument that made a deep impact on my entire way of thinking was when my father said that I was being selfish in wanting to pursue a goal that revolved only around my needs. Here was an opportunity that would enable me to touch other lives. Today, he said, we are making a difference to 50 families. With my participation, we could make a difference to may be 500 families in the near future.

This idea struck a deep chord in my heart. These words goaded me to introspect about the purpose of my life. If I could make a living and at the same time make a difference to so many people by remaining in my country and taking on my father's legacy, then why not, I thought. Creating more employment thus became a big calling for me. Therefore, I decided to join the bandwagon. Till this day, I feel proud that my ambitions are not self-centered and that I am able to give back to the society, albeit in a small way.

From 1999 to 2002, I worked on the shop floor, learning from the ground up and mastered the trade and art of manufacturing. I honed my management acumen and acquired manufacturing and engineering skills. I learnt the ropes of doing business and studied in detail the operations and marketing sections of the business.

Transformation

During these years of 'internship', I developed a clear vision of how I wanted to build this business. Modernization, I realized was the need of the hour. In every industry, modernization is inevitable after a certain point in its life cycle. If you are a small industry and if you are looking at a modest turnover, then traditional methods of doing business will suffice. However, if you are ambitious, to grow, to cater to larger markets, international markets at that, influence a large number of people, then modernization is the driving force. In the 1990's my father had already started exporting our products.

I was ambitious. I wanted our organization to grow. I wanted to establish our organization on foreign soil in a big way. I knew then, that if I didn't transition my business, no matter what the potential is, no matter how many opportunities I get, I couldn't grow.

1. Systematizing

By 2002, I had an understanding of the enormous potential of our business. My father's forte is R&D. His in-depth knowledge of rubber chemistry is the foundation upon which our business operates. Therefore, that was our core strength.

The first important step I took was to put effective systems in place to streamline operations and marketing, the two areas that needed immediate attention. I wanted to bring in the best systems for my organization. I wanted to establish a world-class quality system in the company and I worked towards achieving the ISO/TS 16949 Certification in 2002, making Climax Overseas Private Limited, the first Rubber Component manufacturing company in India to be awarded this certificate. During this implementation I gained a lot of insight into running the company in line with the established systems and it definitely added a lot of value to our marketing.

2. Mechanization/automation

I got actively involved in the business only from 2002. Until such time we were essentially a small skill-based and thus labor-intensive organization with a 60-strong workforce. We had one lady who oversaw accounts. My father did all the R&D. Production was taken care of by employees who were with us for several decades. I always believed in relying on systems than on people to get things done. Therefore, during 2003 and 2004, I started implementing systems that could help in getting more work done.

In 2005, we planned to setup a new plant, I was given the entire responsibility of setting it up from the ground up, and this was a

Greenfield plant. I brought in a lot of technology that was also quite expensive. I introduced Japanese manufacturing practices including KAIZEN, GEMBA, 5S, LEAN MANUFACTURING etc. Without mechanization and automation, volumes cannot be generated. In addition, without volumes, you can neither grow nor can you be competitive in the marketplace and survival would be at stake.

3. Decentralization

In 2005, the new plant was ready. It was 10 times bigger than our previous setup. My father and I were managing every aspect of the business, R&D, procurement, production, marketing and so on. When you are trying to build a huge business, this traditional hierarchical structure can be detrimental. I launched a decentralization exercise. I reorganized the functionality of our business. I created separate departments and streamlined functionality. I appointed department heads. My father was very apprehensive. Being a perfectionist, he was uncertain of how things would shape up without his direct supervision. He always wanted to be involved in every small decision and activity. That's the problem with perfectionists. They do not believe that others could also do a better job until they are shown a lot of proof.

4. Diversification

Growth and sustainability is impossible without diversification. It is one way of coping with the volatility of markets. Your business has to survive despite changes in market requirements, entry of new players, technological innovation etc. Hence, we are investing in many new ventures and starting new product lines to stay ahead.

Having said that the above factors are game changers, we realized while servicing our international clients that in spite of the best systems, latest technology, high-end machinery, it is the quality that finally sustains you in the marketplace.

Breaking Stereotypes

International markets we discovered were averse to doing business with India. Poor quality products and defaulting deadlines by Indian companies had established a strong stereotype about Indian products. So breaking this stereotype and penetrating the market was quite a challenge. Nevertheless, after the initial hiccups, I am proud to say that we always delivered!

I would like to share the fact that we have successfully developed products that other international suppliers could not even dream of. We strive to lead in every market segment that we are a part of. We achieve leadership by understanding what our customers need and then managing our resources to develop, produce and deliver products to not only satisfy the customers but also delight them.

For instance, in 2006, we developed a compound recipe on a formulation for an American client. American suppliers had not been able to achieve the specifications of the client. In fact, researchers from the IITs also said that the specs could not be achieved. My father through his own R&D figured a way to meet this specification. In fact, the product we developed proved to be 40% better than the product they were using from an American supplier. That supplier was a 10-billion dollar turnover group.

Thereafter, we delivered many more specifications that helped us achieve a strong foothold in the international segment and hold a lion's share of the market.

Team Building

One big challenge that I have been facing for quite some time is trying to build a team. Human resource is a very complex and dynamic resource. Of course, a valuable resource too. I learnt early on in my career that investing in human resources and distributing responsibilities among these resources is very essential. If routine operations are taken care of, my father and I could focus on critical issues on the one hand and execute the larger vision of doing business.

I have been very successful in building a team over the past 5 years. This team has shown tremendous interest in taking our vision and mission to the next level. Not always should one look for talent outside. Very often, a little nudge and push can motivate existing talent to push their own limits and perform phenomenally well. So creating a team that thinks and feels in tune with your vision is challenging and I have invested my time on nurturing such a team.

Leadership

Who am I as a leader of my organization?

Demonstrating what I preach - I must set a precedent to what I preach. If I don't adhere to my principles, how can I expect my employees to follow?

Conviction - I will not do anything without conviction and passion. Conviction also comes from a certain level of confidence and faith.

Grit and tenacity - I am very resilient in crisis situations. Nothing can shake me in business. I make sure I think with my mind and not with my heart.

International Exposure

Climax Overseas has a presence today in over 50 countries in 5 continents. Considering that we have a long list of international clientele, I have travelled extensively and have utilized every opportunity to understand different perspectives to do business and work cultures. I have replicated these lessons in my own business.

I must say that I have learnt a lot from the Chinese.

Hospitality
India boasts about how a guest is treated on par with God. However, we are no comparison to Chinese hospitality. For instance, the manner in which they treat their clients is a class apart. The client is chauffeured around in the most luxurious car. A lady accompanies the client. Business usually happens over a luncheon meeting that lasts for about 3-4 hours. The client is treated to a large array of the choicest Chinese delicacies. Lunch and dinner last for hours on end until a certain rapport is built and deals are struck.

Highly Productive Workforce
The Chinese are extremely hard working people. I am not sure if they are culturally ingrained this way or if it is a result of strict labor laws. Their productivity is two to three times more than our own. Although labor is more expensive in China than in India, their winning edge is their high rate of production. Besides, they are ruthlessly punctual when it comes to deliverables. People with a common vision drive the country and that is catalyzing growth in infrastructure and education.

Highly Motivated Female Workforce
Marketing and Sales staffs in most Chinese organizations are usually women. In India, these two areas are still seen as men's forte. In fact, the women work harder than men in China. They are highly trained professional salespersons and make sure the deal is

clinched.

Vision for the Future

We are aiming for exponential growth over the next five years. To speak purely in fiscal terms, we envision a turnover growth from $20 Million to $100 Million.

To translate this vision into reality, we are diversifying, investing in many new ventures and launching new product lines. We are operative in various industries such as automobile, expanding our reach into newer markets, newer industries and newer technologies so that we are able to edge out the competition and keep up the growth momentum.

A passion discovered

Along my growth as an entrepreneur, I inadvertently donned the role of an advisor to friends and associates. They often sought my opinion and counsel on various issues related to work and business. When I look back upon why I was sought after, I realize that my knowledge was real; it came from experience; from trial and error; from learning I made on the floor, in the real world in real-time. It was not just theory. But perhaps theory tested and vetted with experience. I would often go out of my way to advice people on business matters! It never went unsolicited, fortunately! However, if I didn't know the solution or answer, I always openly acknowledge and try to send them in a direction where they can find one.

I made every effort to learn and discover. I am a life-long student. My father, today, at 69 is still a learner. He makes no bones about it. He is constantly updating his knowledge about rubber technology.

For a long time now, I have trained my employees in time-management, negotiations, motivation and other skills. Training has always been an essential mode of updating our workforce. I have also been training other corporate institutions and organizations on these skills. Over the next few years, I would like to focus on this passion for training and build an empire around this. I would like to call myself an infopreneur: imparting my insights on what to do and what not to do in business.

I always emphasize on three prerequisites for an entrepreneur:

Passion - Only if you are passionate about business should you venture into becoming an entrepreneur. In fact, passion is essential to pursue any activity or goal. Do it with passion or not at all. If you are passionate, success follows; hurdles disappear; the course presents itself.

Learn - The capacity to learn is a gift; the ability to learn is a skill; the willingness to learn is a choice. Make sure you are always observing and learning. Mentors, books, seminars, interaction - the scope for learning is enormous.

Invest in people - You can only do only as much as you can do; so you have to build a team around you. No organization is built by one person. You need a team, a workforce that is skilled and passionate enough to take your mission forward.

We have built this empire on the following core values:

- Respect for the Individual, Society and the Environment
- Service to the Customer
- Excellence through Constant Innovation
- Treat all our Product and Service suppliers as Partners in Growth

With these thoughts, I'd like to wish you, the reader, all the very best in your venture and hope I have inspired you to make a positive difference, like the other amazing stories in this book.

Parmeet Singh Sood
Entrepreneur/Author/Speaker/Trainer

Mr. Parmeet Singh Sood has international exposure for the management of SME's having travelled globally and visited many International Companies of various sizes.

Mr. Parmeet Singh Sood spent the first few years in the company working on the shop floor and learning from the ground up and mastered the trade and the art of manufacturing. Combining his management skills and the acquired manufacturing & engineering skills he took the company's manufacturing practices to greater heights by implementing many modern technologies and Japanese Manufacturing practices including KAIZAN, GEMBA, 5S, LEAN MANUFACTURING etc. Also, he headed the endeavor of creating a World Class Quality System in the company and got the company an ISO/TS 16949 Certification in 2002, making Climax Overseas Private Limited the first Rubber Component manufacturing company in India to be awarded this certificate, when industry was practicing an older standard of the now de-funct QS 9000. Given this impetus and vision he put the company on a growth path with annual CAGR of 50%+ in the last 16 years and has made CMX a US$ 20 Million Turnover group in 2015 from what was an under US$ 200,000 company when he joined in 1999. Parmeet Singh Sood's Vision 2020 is to be a US$ 100 million company, a Target which he is passionately pursuing.

Mr. Parmeet Singh Sood has also been a Member of CII's committee for, "Cost Competitiveness in SME's" and successfully organized many seminars for the industry imparting training in the field of Lean Manufacturing and other manufacturing practices. Currently he is leading a Lean Manufacturing Cluster in his Industrial Area and is helping implement Lean Practices in all companies in the cluster. He is an expert on Toyota Production Systems and has been trained by renowned Japanese expert Mr. Mototsugu himself.

Under his leadership, Climax Overseas Pvt. Ltd. has been awarded National Award for Star Performance in Automobile Exports from Ministry of Commerce, Government of India and has been recognized as the fastest growing Export Company in its sector.

Mr. Parmeet Singh Sood has been on a constant journey of learning and growth and has been mentored and trained by some of the top Coaches & Trainers like Rahul Jain (Business Coach), Shiv Khera (Author of International Best Seller You Can Win), T. Harv Ecker (Author of Secrets of the Millionaire Mind), Blair Singer, Alex Mandossian, Robert Riopel, Courtney Smith to name a few.

Mr. Parmeet Singh Sood himself is an avid trainer in the field of Manufacturing Process Improvements, Quality Systems, Stock Trading & Investments and his latest passion on Manifestation (Signature Program: Awaken the Genie in You!). Over the last few years Mr. Sood has trained more than 1000 professionals in various fields on various industry platforms.

Mr Sood has been invited to various industry body seminars and conferences as a Keynote Speaker and he loves going back to his alma mater and speaks with the students on entrepreneurship.

2

THE ROAD LESS TRAVELED

- BY RAJESH DEMBLA, TECH ENTREPRENEUR

The cactus is a metaphor for life. In spite of everything, it survives in the most severe & ruthless of conditions.

Well, why do I start on this note? My story is that of a young boy who lost everything, his home, his family, and relatives. However, I never gave up on myself & charted my own life.

My childhood has been one of loss and struggle. We were a large family of 35 people, living under a single roof. Getting two square meals a day was what we struggled for. On hindsight, I attribute the poverty and struggle to lack of education. None in my family was formally educated. Education was not a priority. Nevertheless, I enjoyed school. I looked forward to going to school, I liked to learn. That thirst for learning, for knowledge has been my saving grace.

I was a topper in class. I dreamt of studying engineering. I even nursed the ambition of studying to an Ivy League institution! Until I turned 12. Two incidents changed my life irrevocably. I was totally thrown off gear. The 105-year-old ancestral house in which we lived was destroyed in a torrential rain. I was in the house when the building collapsed. I remember being rescued and looking at the collapsed rumbles not knowing what will happen to me or my family. Next I lost my father a month later. It was like as if the world had come to an end. I just lived with no purpose for the next 3 years. Every time I saw my friends living a secured life with parents to care for them, I wondered what wrong had I done to deserve this.

My lesson: Both these incidents made me realize that nothing is certain or permanent.

By 15, I completed my 10th grade and was told by my mother that we cannot afford for me to go to college. If I wanted to, I need to do it on my own, while I also support the family financially. I had to immediately look for a job. That happened, I landed a job. I was so elated, that I didn't bother to find out the nature of work I was expected to do. The next morning when I went to work I found out my job profile - **office boy**; sweep, mop the floor, fill up water, clean the office, fetch breakfast for employees, clean plates - that was my job description. I could have quit and run, but I knew this would fetch me a salary that would suffice for a college admission fee. I swallowed my pride and took everything that was thrown at me. I survived.

My Lesson: Focus of your goal, no matter what you go through, as long as you achieve what you want to.

Finally, I paid up the admission fee and started college as a morning batch student. I attended college from 7am to 11 am and worked for the rest of the day. However, the money I earned barely met the family's needs. Therefore, I worked night shifts as well. Soon money gained priority over education and I quit college. I was disillusioned.

I stopped going home at night. I slept in the Bangalore Railway Station. I did this for three months. Strangely, absurdly amidst the squalor of my life, a dream germinated in my heart. Was it an escape strategy? I dreamt of owning a bungalow, a Mercedes Benz; of travelling the world; of building my own business. I started to dream BIG. While I was surrounded by street urchins, anti-social elements, corrupt cops and unmentionable activities my only goals were to achieve respect, fame and wealth. I mentioned this to some friends and acquaintances, only to be laughed at. They would say "dreams are just dreams, they will never happen in reality"

Every time I was laughed at, it made me stronger and I told myself, I will achieve it, no matter how long it takes, or how much I have to fight.

My Lesson: Adverse conditions will bring out the best in you, stay strong and persistent.

At this point I quit college and searched for a full-time job. I applied to a company called GetIt Yellow Pages, which published a business directory of the same name. A relatively new concept in India, the company or its product was barely known. I went for the interview knowing that I am not a graduate and my chances of getting the job were "nil". Since I had nothing to lose, I was at my cynical best during the interaction with the interviewer. At the end of half an hour, I was offered the job! I owned up immediately that I had lied about my qualification in my resume! He did not change his mind.

My Lesson: Nothing is impossible if you believe in yourself, you just need to try, even if it is out of your reach.

Marriage:

When I was going through this struggle, I met Mamtha and we instantly clicked. She was 18 and I was 21 when we got married. Kind of unimaginable to marry that early, but it just happened. She has been my biggest support in life. The kind of sacrifices she has made to stand by me in all circumstances has been awesome. I don't think I would have survived or fared well if not for her. I want to specially thank her for this amazing companionship. Its 25 years since we have been married and have two amazing kids, Raunak and Mihika.

At Yellow Pages

I was offered the opportunity to go to Coimbatore where the company was opening a new branch. A new city, without knowing a word of Tamil (the regional language) If I agreed to work there for three months, I was offered a raise and promotion back in Bangalore. I took up the offer.

At first I failed miserably for 2 weeks, I was unable to get a single sale. In spite of working sincerely, I could not perform, that's when I started observing the local people and I realized I was different. I started to learn their language. Every prospective customer I would meet, I would not talk about selling my product, but ask them to teach me their language. They loved it! They would start buying on their own. I had discovered the formula.

My Lesson: Blend in or get out

There was no looking back, the 3 month stint ended with me as the Top performer in the entire region. I got back to Bangalore and outperformed all the seniors and earned a couple of promotions too.

Around this time another dream came true, I was hand-picked by the Management to go to Philippines with 3 others from the management to study certain processes and implement them in India. I also visited Singapore, Dubai among others and gained good exposure of international markets.

During these years I met many Canadians, Americans and Japanese top management Executives of Bell Canada, GTE, Nippon Directories etc. They would visit India and be treated like Gods by the Board of our company. I always wondered, if I would ever experience that in my life? Would I ever reach a position of a national head or handle International operations? But dream, I would….

Within 2 years I was rated the Top Performer and at the end of 7 years I was promoted as Head of Operations. During this span, I saw the best and worst of corporate life.

A specific period during this stint stands out, I was reporting to a boss who was very insecure. He would try to put me down even time. He would say, "Rajesh, you will never get promoted, you will never achieve anything worth in life" He would insult me at every given opportunity, I would feel very bad. Even though I felt I was better than him, he was designated higher and was my boss. I finally could not take it anymore and on one such instance, I gave it back in a nice way. I told him that in the next 6 months, I will be on par with him and soon, he would report to me.

It was a tall claim, I had no idea how I would do it, but I wanted it real bad. In 1993 July, I did something extra-ordinary; I completed 1 year's target in one month. I worked like as if I was possessed.

Finally, I was promoted. I was on par with him, and within the next 1 year, I got another promotion, and unfortunately for him, he had to report to me.

I felt really good but I knew he would be feeling miserable, so I did make it a point to treat him nicely and work towards his betterment. We became friends and that we are till now.

I would remember the nights on the Railway platform a few years ago and feel good that I had made it this far. However, I was hungry for more. My dreams were bigger.

By 1997, I realized the organization was not keeping pace with the evolving market conditions and technology. It was difficult but I decided to quit without another job in hand.

My Lesson: Your heart knows best, listen to it.

First brush with Justdial

One day I was watching an interview on CNBC. A gentleman named V.S.S Mani was talking about a concept very similar to yellow pages, not as a book; but as a service leveraging technology - the computer and the telephone. This was round about the time India was witnessing the telecom revolution. At that moment I knew that if Mani's concept takes off, then it would sound the death knell for the paper based telephone directories i.e., yellow pages.

As if by providence, Mani's brother got in touch with me & sought my assistance in setting up Justdial in Bangalore. However,

I didn't want to work for someone else anymore. The desire to start my own venture was taking wings. I joined Justdial as a franchisee and set up the business side of the venture.

Within a year Justdial was a pan India Company. The growth rate was mind blowing, in 1999 - 2000 Mani had sold Justdial to indiainfo.com and I decided to move away at that time.

Start of the Internet Era

The world was changing, from Silicon Valley in the USA to Bangalore in India, Dotcom's were getting funded and it looked as if the entire world is turning on its head. There were talks of newspapers and television becoming obsolete, and how internet will help people do everything online.

In 1999, one evening I got a phone call, it was from someone I did not know. She asked me if I would like to be the first Indian to set up a Yellow Pages Online. Instantly I felt I should, it was a calling.

I got an offer to join Indya.com as a channel producer and publish India's first online Yellow pages. Like I said, I grabbed it. This perhaps is one of the best decisions I made. I was able to plan & create a world class product with pan India operations. The kind of people I worked with was awesome. This assignment taught me more than I had ever learnt in my life, I managed P&L's, hiring, training, product, content, market strategy, pricing, practically everything. It was a dream come true! It was like going to an Ivy league university. Working with a leader like Sunil Lulla who was the CEO of indya.com has been one of the most amazing learning experiences of my life.

In 2001, India reeled under the impact of the global IT collapse. Indya.com was shutdown. I however had grown richer with the experience and learning at Indya.com.

My Lesson: Nothing lasts forever, keep moving!
Back to Justdial

During the Global IT collapse, even indiainfo.com shut down, Mani bought back Justdial, because he still had faith in his concept, his decision to buy back Justdial increased my respect for him manifold for two reasons; his unflinching faith in an idea and his vision. If not for Mani, Justdial would not have been what it is today.

The next 13 years were something that I will cherish all my life. I worked with Mani, who in my opinion was the most focused entrepreneur, a visionary. He was thinking about building a parallel to Google in India, but for local search.

In 2002, when I was invited to be part of Justdial, I didn't think twice. All that mattered at that point was the challenge that was awaiting me.

Justdial's presence was limited to a few cities in India, our first goal was to set up operations all over India and market it nationally, we needed to invest in infrastructure, people etc. Justdial looked for funding but in vain.

The Venture Funding scene was very different those days, Call centers were thriving. We also had a call-center, but a captive one, many potential investors suggested to us to turn Justdial into a call center/BPO business for the US market and they would gladly fund it. Thankfully Mani and the rest of us stuck to our belief in the concept of Justdial.

Business was growing by word of mouth. Users kept increasing by the day and we kept expanding into newer cities. We grew organically, but we had a peculiar problem. We were not yet a brand to reckon with. People knew that they had to call a certain telephone number but they didn't know that they were calling Justdial. To build a brand we needed a full-fledged brand building exercise, which required huge funding, but that was not happening.

We had to think out of the box, we had to market ourselves nationally without money. We did the unthinkable and decided to launch a printed Yellow Pages and called it Justdial Yellow Pages. Even though the publications were dying a slow death, as they were being disrupted by digital ones, we decided to pursue this option with a clear vision to achieve 2 things

1. Brand Visibility amongst Small medium Businesses in the country
2. At Zero cost and yet be profitable

I was asked to head the venture as "Country Head" in 2004. The day Mani called me and asked if could head this, I remembered my days at the Railway platform and all those who said that dreams don't come true, I also remembered my boss of one time, who had said I will never achieve anything in life, well… they were wrong !! Weren't they?

Now, I got a chance to create a Yellow Pages of my own. It was exciting and scary. We were about to take Tata Yellow pages and Getit Yellow Pages (My previous employer) head on. They were giants and had become house hold names in the country. I knew only one thing, I need to focus on our goals and emerge at the top.

The fact that the entire sales force of Justdial from 1997 to 2004 had been telling every small business in the country not to list on the printed Yellow Pages, rather be on Justdial did not help either. Now, we would have to go back to the same businesses and say list on our yellow pages.

I needed a team to do this, all I got from the existing employees was 2 people, I had to recruit an army and get them to do this on my own.

Within a span of three years we built a very profitable business from the print product alone; we set up a team of 600 people; we contributed almost 40% of the overall company's revenues; we had put in place a zero capital brand building exercise with an outreach of 2.5 million businesses, having the Justdial brand on their desks for years.

By then the usage of the voice product had grown significantly too. Revenues were growing at more than 40% year on year. Our success was recognized by the industry and investors started walking into our office for the first time. In 2006, Justdial got funded by Saif Partners followed by Tiger Global, and Sequoia, and the rest is history.

High touch, low-tech to High touch, high-tech company

Sandipan Chattopadhyay joined Justdial as CTO (chief technology officer). Both Sandipan and I had joined as external vendors and in our own ways changed the face and the fortunes of the company. My personal view is that Justdial had a pre Sandipan and post Sandipan era. He built the technology that transformed the way we worked, the way users used Justdial. His contribution impacted the productivity of every employee and propelled Justdial to great heights. Of course, all of this under the able leadership of Mani, who I regard as an entrepreneur par excellence and a visionary.

In 2009, Mani wanted to go global and establish Justdial in UK, US, Australia and other English speaking countries. The printed

Justdial Yellow Pages had served its purpose of establishing brand recall and had now become obsolete. Therefore, it was discontinued in 2009; the web version, Justdial.com flourished. We decided to replicate the voice and web model in the US with a core team comprising Mani, his brother and me.

What Works Here, May Not Work There

In 2010, I moved to the US entity to launch Justdial's international operations. However, not much could be achieved, some of the reasons in my opinion are

- We replicated the India model in the US. Replication in itself is not a bad idea. However, we also executed the operations from India. We should have had Americans answering the calls rather than Indian's. The average Amercian did not like talking to a foreigner when he had a choice of paid 411 who understood him better. Although, leveraging the existing infrastructure to service the American market made sense in terms of economics, it did not bridge the cultural chasm between the two countries.

- Right from the start, we focused on pan-America operations. That required huge capital. We didn't have that kind of money. We should have started small; focused on a single city, maybe New York with an American call center.

- The Indian wing of Justdial was ready to go public and our energies were more focused on that.

Although the US operation did not do well, it gave me an insight into how things work in different parts of the world and I met some of the most amazing people like Marshall Goldsmith.

Since we lived in the same building, I bumped into him. He gave me a personally signed copy of his newly launched book What Got You Here, Won't Get You There. That had a huge impact on my decision making for the future. I want to thank Marshall for all the wisdom and insights he shared with me.

Innovation, the mantra for survival and growth

While there was jubilation over Justdial's success in terms of the hugely successful IPO and the rise in share price from roughly $10 to $30 in India, I was constantly aware that we were not innovating. My personal opinion was that the next level of growth would have come with mergers, acquisitions and fulfilment in the true sense. We probably were missing out and allowing verticals like Ola, Uber, Zomato, Swiggy etc to gain ground.

Sometime in 2014 our valuation in India was about $2 billion. Which was amazing considering that Mani started this company with just $1,000.

However, that did not last and the valuations and relevance of Just dial started to see a drop.

Flying Solo

From September 2012 I had started feeling that the eco system around us is changing, I would follow Mary Meeker's "Global Internet Trends" report and realized that I should get involved with a few tech start up's. That's when I got involved with mentoring Solutions Infini Technologies; it was a bunch of young boys out of college and were clocking about 200,000 USD in top line. With all that I had learnt, I started spending some Saturdays to help strategize their business and in 5 years, today they are clocking close to 20Million USD per annum, with clients across Asia, Europe and Africa. The company has won the Deloitte Fast 50 in

India and Asia for 3 years in a row.

I became very passionate about mentoring start-ups. I aimed to be part of many start-ups! However, I was clear in my head that I didn't want to own a company 100% rather own small stakes in all of them. I just wanted to work with people who are young, energetic, enthusiastic, willing to take risks, to innovate/disrupt and nurture dreams that are greater than making money. Most importantly, I wanted to work with people with no EGO.

During this period I would share my feelings with two of my colleagues, Sandipan the CTO and Srinivas the Deputy CFO of Justdial. Both of them were also planning to move out and start something of their own. Obviously they had their own reasons to move out of Justdial. The 3 of us decided that we would join hands and start something together. Sandipan had coined the word "Xelpmoc" which is a sort of palindrome for "Complex". We were sure that we would turn anything that was complex, around. Be it technology, product, marketing, strategy, financial planning, data and analytics, we did not want to do run of the mill stuff.

Forming Xelpmoc

In March 2015, I resigned from Justdial. & got relieved in August. Shortly after that we founded "Xelpmoc" with a vision to build an incubator for startups that actually walked the talk.

What were the problems we saw in the startup eco system?

More than 95% of the startups were failing, because of a few reasons:

Technology - Many of the startups had very effective business strategies, but the technology team was unable to deliver on time and there was a gap between the plans and the actual product.

Why was this happening?

Finding tech talent was difficult. If they did find talent, retaining them was difficult. Keeping them interested in the product beyond a reasonable time frame was another challenge.

Easily available funding from the VC and PE world, added to the problem. Good techie's were being offered astronomical salaries and poached by other companies.

There was a lack of learning opportunities for techies, as they would only work on solving limited challenges and therefore leave for more challenging opportunities.

Another unique problem that we noticed was, the entrepreneurs who were failing were usually Techies with lack of business know how or the other way around – Business experts with lack of tech know how. Most of them were also at a loss with compliance, financial management, brand strategy, marketing etc and would resort to outsourcing critical functions in exchange for a fee or hire people in house, who would leave as soon as they got another opportunity.

The companies to whom these jobs were outsourced, were more interested in the fee than the success of the startup over all, so they worked on a brief and would hardly do more than that.

So what was the answer?

What if entrepreneurs could find a "co-founder" who would come in with the entire set of resources that were required and have skin in the game, what if this co-founder would invest his time, money and resources but would make money when the venture is successful. And what if this co-founder was a large team of highly talented people, across all functions.

That is "Xelpmoc"

We are a team of very high caliber techies including Data Scientists, UI and UX experts, developers, IOS and Android experts, Testers, AI specialists, Solution Architects etc. On the non-tech side, we have experts in Marketing – traditional and digital, branding and positioning, MIS, analytics experts and financial management experts. We have handpicked people that valued creativity. We believe we have put together a team of mavericks who work on projects because they love the idea and only if they like the entrepreneur's vision. Every team member gets to work on products that interest them.

At Xelpmoc we are incubating companies in several domains – Healthcare, Education, Fintech, IoT, Big Data, Logistics, Supply Chain Management etc.

How do we work with our teams?

Apart from salaries the team gets part of the equity that we get in every project, we share 35% with the team that works on the project and contributes to its success. It is based on a mathematical formula and allows for a fair chance to get equity only on high quality continued contribution method. This ensures that the team stays focused on the success of the business at all times.

Validation of our business model

When we started, there was a lot of interest from budding entrepreneurs to work with us. But we were cognizant of the fact that validation would happen when a large VC/PE or a world renowned Technocrat would want to work with us. We also wanted to see if Entrepreneurs from more developed markets would like to work in this model.

All of this has happened!!!!

It is under year and we have built and launched products that have been funded by the likes of Mr.Nandan Nilekani and Accel Partners. Entrepreneurs from UK and Singapore have started working with us. It has been like a dream run.

For me the journey at Xelpmoc has just begun, I wake up every morning excited to go to work, I love the energy. I am happy that I am doing what I want to do.

Looking back and connecting the dots

When I look back at my life, I have been drawn to start ups from the beginning, Getit Yellow Pages, Justdial, indya.com were all startups when I joined them. Each of them was a giant in its own respect when I decided to move out to find something more meaningful. Each time, I have found myself in a better position, when I have quit the comfort zone.

I must admit, the decision to quit a comfortable job in a very well established business at its peak has been tough, especially when you have been a crucial part of building it from scratch. But it has turned out to be the right one for me.

I connect well with Robert Frost, when he says,
Two roads diverged in a wood, and I—
I took the one less traveled by,
And that has made all the difference.

Disclaimer: All views shared here are my personal views and

experiences, they are not intended to promote or malign any individual, business or brand. Factual errors if any are regretted.

Rajesh Dembla

Mr Rajesh dembla is the Founder and Managing Director of Xelpmoc design and Tech - A path breaking concept in the world of Technology and Start Ups. He has and continues to incubate and co found ventures in various domains that touch human lives everyday. He has keen interests in Fintech, Health care, IOT, Logistics, Education, AI, Search etc.

He holds stake in companies across India, UK and Singapore and is keen to explore the US start up eco system. Rajesh has been instrumental in the growth of many start ups in India. He advises and mentors them on Strategy, Brand Building, Geo planning, Technology adoption, Customer acquisition and Change Management.

Prior to this venture, Mr Rajesh Dembla was Group Vice

President of Justdial Ltd, handling Global operations. He was part of Just dial from an early struggle phase to funding from marquee Investors like SAIF Partners, Tiger Global, Sequoia etc and then Public Listing on the Indian Stock Exchange. He was an integral part of the team that led the organically grown Just Dial to become a unicorn. He has helmed the Just dial Yellow Pages and played a key role in taking the company to International markets.

Before Just dial Rajesh was a Channel Producer at Indya.com, which was funded by Mr Rupert Murdoch, Chase capital etc. He became the first Indian to create an Online Yellow Pages in India in theyear 1999 - 2000.

Starting his structured career from Getit Yellow Pages at the age of 21 without any formal education, Rajesh played a key role in making Getit a house hold brand in India.

Mr Rajesh Dembla has been featured by the Corporate Citizen, Business World and several other publications. He has also been invited to speak at many B Schools, Colleges and Universities in India. He loves to spend time with students and is ever willing to share all that he knows with them.

Mr Rajesh Dembla is Married to Mamtha and they have 2 Kids. He has candidly said the support his family has provided has been the reason he could dream and go after his dreams.

Website: Xelpmoc.in
Linkedin - https://www.linkedin.com/in/rajesh-dembla
Email - rajesh@xelpmoc.in

3

UNBRIDLED IMAGINATION

- BY THUMBAY MOIDEEN, FOUNDER OF THUMBAY GROUP

Perhaps, the defining factor of my life and every journey I have embarked upon thus far, is to strike roots deep into what I am and then spread my wings and fly high to discover what more I can be. My evolution as a businessman on foreign soil despite rooted in my land of birth and its culture, is illustration enough.

Striking Roots

I was born and brought up in Mangalore, Karnataka, India. I come from a large joint family, in which every member was a successful businessman in his own right. During my younger formative years, I was strongly influenced by my family who were shrewd businessmen as much as they nurtured and valued family ties and relationships. A culture of ethical conduct of business, generosity, big heartedness and godliness was ingrained in us at a young age. In my perspective, a holistic and strong cultural environment is the foundation upon which successful and long-lasting business empires are built. This is the most important family legacy that I have resolutely passed on to my children.

My paternal grandfather owned a shipping business and my maternal grandfather ran a timber business. In 1978, at the age of 21 I made my foray in the world of business and took over my father's thriving timber business. I remember my father objecting to my rigorous working schedule even then. Nevertheless, I wouldn't slow down my pace. I had to reach my goals.

Stepping Stone

I consolidated the timber business in India and expanded it to the markets in the Middle East. In 1997, I perceived a huge opportunity in real estate in Ajman, where I was able to acquire several buildings on lease and started off with rental and leasing business, even as the assured growth rates were phenomenal.

The turning point in my life and career was a chance encounter with the ruling family of Ajman. Once on my way to Africa, I had to transit through Dubai. I had a chance encounter with a member of the ruling family. We discussed the economy of Ajman and ways to develop and boost it. During this discussion, I told him about how a small town near Mangalore transformed into a prominent hub for medical education after a medical college was set up by a visionary businessman. I casually stated that establishing a medical school could generate innumerable opportunities for the economy of Ajman.

A few days later I was invited to meet the Ruler of Ajman who proposed a request to set up a medical school in Ajman. By the grace of Almighty, I was able to set up the Thumbay Group in the UAE and we founded the Gulf Medical College (presently Gulf Medical University). This project in many ways was a launch pad for Thumbay Group's diversification into multiple industrial segments. After this there was no looking back.

Medical Education

Since my expertise lay in timber and real estate business, I sought permission to hire a few consultants from India before proceeding with the project. I recruited a few consultants from top-notch universities, and after thorough market research and analysis, we unanimously concluded that there is huge scope for a medical university in Ajman.

I required support in three fundamental areas and the same was conveyed to His Highness. Firstly, Ministry of Higher Education doesn't allow expats to own a license for institutions catering to higher education. Secondly, I needed approximately 25 acres of land to build the college. Thirdly, I required a hospital to train our students.

The Ajman Government catered to my first requirement by awarding me a royal decree for the formation of the Gulf Medical College. The process of accreditation was prolonged over 7 years. His Highness resolved my second obstacle by gifting me 25 acres (1 million sq. ft.) of land. When I approached the bank to mortgage the land, they refused as it was gifted. They suggested I buy it from the government. I did the same. We were targeting Asian students but we enrolled students from 30 different countries. As soon as the students graduated and had to practice at Khalifa Hospital, the authorities objected saying the hospital couldn't accommodate so many students. I had no other option but to build a hospital. In the early 2000s, we built a 200-bed hospital, which was a huge accomplishment in itself.

Besides, to convince the Ministry of Health, UAE that an Indian company could run and sustain a university of this stature on foreign soil, without compromising on the quality of education was a challenge. Fortunately, within 3 years GMU students were being recruited for internship by major government run hospitals all over UAE. More importantly our own conviction had to be consolidated. The motive for setting up GMU was to serve the large expatriate student community in the UAE. However, the applications in the first year itself proved that we were well received and that the university was providing a fertile environment for students from diverse cultures and nationalities to thrive.

Today, GMU has emerged as the most sought after private medical university in the region, attracting students from as many as 73 nationalities and, faculty and staff from over 22 nationalities.

But I could not sit back and gloat over the success of this institution alone. Excelling in one field is a safe strategy. I told myself that this is just the beginning and that I have a long way to go. As Arthur Ashe has said, 'Success is a journey not a destination. The doing is often more important than the outcome.'

Taking Wings – Diversification

Motivated by our success in the medical education field and with a better understanding of the business environment of UAE, we launched ourselves into several fields, both allied and diverse.

With intent to be holistically involved in the healthcare industry, we established hospitals, and involved ourselves in research and diagnostics, wellness, nutrition and pharmacy. The Thumbay hospitals are currently operational in Ajman, Dubai, Fujairah, Sharjah and India, and are being managed by my elder son Akbar, a fourth generation entrepreneur. The highlight of our hospital chain, apart from the core world-class facility and service, is that services are being offered to patients from 175 nationalities in 50 languages! We have opened clinics and pharmacies in almost all the Emirates of UAE.

Apart from healthcare, we set foot into the construction and hospitality segments. The initial phase of diversification was rather unsettling as we were venturing into unchartered territories. But we were not guided by factors that defied business acumen and did not do anything impulsively. We planned extensively, played strategically and took calculated risks.

Our hospitality segment comprises a chain of restaurants, coffee shops and health clubs and spas. My daughter-in-law, Nousheen manages the bi-monthly magazine that focuses on health and lifestyle, as well as the flower shop business.

The real-estate wing, which constitutes a sizable portion of the Thumbay Group is managed by my younger son Akram. We have a large clientele in India and UAE, especially in the northern part of UAE. We provide a host of services such as planning, designing and execution.

The cornerstone of my business philosophy has always been innovation. Innovate, Adapt and Reinvent - these three strategies have helped me build and sustain the Thumbay group. It is easy to start any enterprise, but to sustain is the greater challenge. This is perhaps the greatest lesson I have learned in my career. So we persevered and never gave into complacency.

Another principle I have never compromised upon is quality, be it in product or service. A robust business plan is always customer-oriented. Building confidence in the market is part of a long-term business plan. It helps build confidence, satisfaction, trust and loyalty among the community across cultures.

For any business to thrive, I think, a favorable economic and political environment is indispensible. Besides, a businessman is fortunate if he can build a good support team. I owe the success of every organization of the Thumbay group to the people who are at its helm and all the others who make it work at the ground level. They are the driving force behind the Thumbay group.

Having said that, there is no growth without hurdles and setbacks. Time and again we were faced with challenging situations, but we have developed a work culture at Thumbay Group that keeps us committed to our goal and powers us with the zeal to stick to our guns until the goal is reached.

Focus determines Reality

My generation of entrepreneurs have learnt the nuances of running a business the difficult way. We have walked the path, faltered, fallen, struggled and we have walked again. Although today's generation face a higher level of competition and respond well to challenges, they need to be further nurtured and molded; taught grit and courage. I cannot stress the need for focus. I read George Lucas say, 'Focus is what determines reality'.

In my talks and interactions with budding and aspiring young entrepreneurs, I caution them against setting average ambitions and settling down in their comfort zones. I always emphasize to them, the need to 'dream big to be big'. A ship in a harbor is safe. However, that's not what ships are built for.

Fortunately, my children are the bastions of my legacy. The tripod upon which to build success, I tell my children, as I would like to convey to all young ambitious entrepreneurs are imagination, ethics and hard work. Imbibe the power of unbridled imagination to dream big and evolve an organic vision to translate dreams to reality. Moreover, needless to say, there is no alternative to hard work and to remain grounded at all times.

I have ingrained the culture of ethical path to success. I do not want my institutions to be money-minting machines. So being ruthless or resorting to unethical practices to mint money isn't my intention. To illustrate this point, we deal with over 40 insurance companies from across the region, which have sent mystery shoppers to our hospitals. Last year, some insurance companies stated that there was no need to send mystery shoppers to our hospitals anymore. I think this says it all. We have incurred losses but we have never manipulated anything or anybody nor have we resorted to unethical practices. It's very simple. The easiest way to do business is the straight path not the convoluted, crooked path.

Going Global

My vision is literally to go places. I want to make Thumbay group a leading business house with a global presence. To establish ourselves on foreign shores demands a strong set of values that foster business integration while creating a sense of belonging. These values should hold good irrespective of business areas, the existing corporate culture of the country and the country of operation.

Travelling the world to expand my business has been a great mentor. I amassed immeasurable knowledge. Your mind becomes sensitive to cultures nuances, behavioral etiquettes, people management etc.

Future Plans

Over the past 16 years, we have established operations in 13 sectors. We are spread across India and Ghana and plans are afoot to expand to South Asia, Africa and the rest of UAE. We have received proposals from several countries to set up campuses, hospitals and research facilities.

We have a fairly good presence in India particularly in the construction centre. We will shortly open coffee shops and wellness spas in Indian metros too. We have recently opened Thumbay New Life Hospital at Hyderabad and plan to start five more in major metros. GMU is also working on setting up a university in India.

The following values drive our business:
Excellence: Provide customers with a consistently high level of service through continuous benchmarking of operations and realigning of processes.

Trust: Ensure trust and respect for business success through open communication, dialogue and delegation of responsibilities.

Knowledge: Interact closely with customers by creating and sharing knowledge that adds value and is relevant.

Innovation: Pursue innovation so as to harness cutting edge technology, using insights to invent a better future that makes healthcare serve fairly, productively and consistently.

Integrity: Ensure the highest levels of personal and institutional ethics and integrity, make honest commitments and work to consistently honor them.

On hindsight/In retrospection I think my growth chart as a human being and as a business man can be mapped based on the three most important decisions I made in my life: first, my decision to marry Zohra, my life partner; I couldn't have asked for a better companion; second, to migrate to the beautiful land of United Arab Emirates; lastly, venturing into education and healthcare sectors.

My father, Mr. B. Ahmed Haji Mohiudeen and my wife Zohra have taught me the most important lessons of life, which no business school can teach. My father taught me to understand and value the worth of what we have. My wife, the pillar of my strength, made me realize that life is not about running to reach the next milestone; life is about living in the moment and playing our part with diligence in the phenomenal scheme of things. Being with my family, is my way of anchoring with my own self. Such a realization brings in great humility. I cherish the time I spend with my grand children. I occasionally lose myself in a good book or even a movie.

Awards, recognitions and accolades come and go. They motivate me to excel further. Nevertheless, all things said and done, I sincerely believe that the number of lives you are able to touch; reach and make a difference measures success. It would be cowardice on my part to shirk away from fulfilling my social responsibility.

It is humility that drives Thumbay group in all its philanthropic activities. For us philanthropy is a duty to society and an act of giving back rather than an act of charity. The Thumbay Foundation, set up as a charitable trust, is being ably managed by my wife Zohra. The Foundation provides scholarships, grants, bursaries, awards, fellowships, endowments, donations and other forms of financial assistance to deserving students pursuing education or training. The group has also spearheaded Sponsor-a-Medical- Professional whereby the Gulf Medical University gives scholarship to deserving, meritorious students to pursue a medical course in the subject of their choice. Thumbay group's hospitals have a dedicated Patient's Affairs Department, which provides treatment at subsidized rates, to ensure that a patient is not denied healthcare, because of economic concerns. Free medical camps are also conducted for the public at regular intervals.

Thumbay Moideen

A man of vision and dynamism with a determination to succeed, Thumbay Moideen is recognized in India and beyond, for the various achievements to his credit.

He was born on 23 March 1957 in Mangalore, Karnataka. A third generation entrepreneur from a well-known business family from Mangalore, at the age of 21 years he took over the reins of the large business house established by his father.

Thumbay Moideen brought the family business to the Persian Gulf with the launch of the Thumbay Group, UAE (United Arab Emirates) in 1998. He established the Gulf Medical University, which ultimately became a destination for medical education for students from over 73 countries. Today, Thumbay Group has developed into a business conglomerate with diversified business operations in 14 sectors including healthcare, education, research, diagnostics, retail pharmacy, health communications, publishing, retail opticals, wellness, hospitality, information technology, trading, distribution and real estate, spread out across the UAE as well as other countries. The Group today employs close to 4000 people, which will rise to 6000 with the completion of ongoing projects and to 15,000 employees by the end of 2020.

Thumbay Moideen has been bestowed with various awards and recognitions in the UAE and abroad. He has consistently been on the 'most influential' and 'top leaders' lists published by reputed international publications. He was recently featured on the cover of Forbes Middle East.

He has been an invited speaker at various international conferences and seminars held in America, Europe, Middle East and the Indian subcontinent. He has also been invited by various associations and organizations to be on their board as an active office bearer or in an advisory capacity.

Moideen is married to Zohra Moideen and has two sons, Akbar Moideen Thumbay and Akram Moideen Thumbay. Akbar manages Thumbay Group's hospitals as the Vice President of the healthcare division, while Akram manages the construction & renovation division as its Director-Operations. Akbar is married to Nousheen Salma, who is in charge of handling the editorial and design advice of 'Health' magazine, Thumbay Group's health and lifestyle publication.

PARMEET SINGH SOOD

4

EMBRACE CHANGE
MANIFESTING MY REALITY BY CREATING BUDLI

- BY ROHIT BAGARIA, FOUNDER OF BUDLI.IN

"All the world's a stage,
And all the men and women merely players;
They have their exits and their entrances,
And one man in his time plays many parts,
His acts being seven ages."

These lines from Shakespeare share a deep semblance to my story.

Writing a book has been on my bucket list for some time. It is a channel to express my thoughts, share my story and hopefully inspire someone to follow their dreams.

"To follow knowledge like a sinking star, beyond the utmost bound of human thought."

Growing up, I've been passionate about three things - Lego, travel, and technology. I am a creator and I've always loved creating. My hobby since the age of 7 was collecting airline timetables & studying airline routes. I used to write to airlines around the world and they would send me their timetables. My childhood dream was to have my own airline.

Schooling was enjoyable as I used to enjoy learning. I used to do well in subjects where the teacher had the ability to retain my attention. In my humble opinion, intelligence is just a level of curiosity.

I took a big hit when I was 19. My hip joints had gotten fused and I was in excruciating pain and could not move for 2 years. A surgery enabled me to lead a normal life thereafter. This period of struggle taught me resilience, perseverance, grit, fearlessness and self-belief in overcoming all challenges. I was so dependent on others for everything that I swore to never be dependent on anyone ever again.

Introduced to technology at an early age, I had an affinity for computers. Initially, I enjoyed playing games on it. However, the introduction of the Internet opened up a new world to me. I could not find any website with information on airlines, so I figured out how to build my own website with this information compiled. Something which I did for fun got featured in The Times of India, a leading Indian newspaper, and to my surprise, I started getting advertisement offers on it.

However, I did not pursue it as I decided to go to UC Berkeley, California for further studies. Being in the Bay Area and meeting people from around the world was thoroughly enriching. Working at a software startup in Silicon Valley proved to be a useful learning experience. It opened my mind to new thoughts, ideas, and possibilities which would not have been possible otherwise. What struck me the most was the cultural difference in the attitude towards failure. I learned that failure was a part of success and one cannot succeed without failing.

Experience is what you get when you don't get what you want.

I wanted to stay back in the US but came back to India to join my family business as my father had suddenly passed away and I felt it was my moral responsibility towards the family legacy. The business was a pioneer in manufacturing and international sales across 35 countries, started by my grandfather. However, I did not enjoy it as I was not passionate about it. I am a creator and I wanted to experience the thrill of creating something new. Numerous differences with my family arose on how to run the business and I did not appreciate the prevailing company culture. I figured that my time is limited. I needed to do something purposeful which I really enjoyed. I wanted to play a larger game.

When I wanted to branch out to do something on my own, having no support from my family made me even more determined. I had no capital and was living in an environment of negativity. It was a difficult period when I went through a broken relationship, financial, social and emotional turmoil. During my struggles, my sister has been the rock who I could always rely on for support. Someone came into my life who had a profound impact on me, changed my perspective and taught me gratitude.

We are the sum of five people who are closest to us. It is very important that we choose these people wisely as they are the ones who will either help us grow or pull us back. I made a conscious decision to distance myself from people who were pulling me back and only choose those who are full of positivity and help me grow.

The most delightful surprise in life is to suddenly recognize your own worth.

Desperate to find answers, I stumbled upon *Vipassana* meditation. I had no idea about it as I was never previously introduced or inclined towards any form of spirituality or meditation. I decided to go for it with an open mind and just two objectives - to complete the program and do it to the best of my ability. This is where I felt the divine energy within me.

Kairos **- A moment within a moment where drastic change takes place.**

The most important journey that any of us would ever undertake is the journey within ourselves. This was the beginning of my awakening and spiritual journey. It changed my perspective completely. I realized that we are not human beings having a spiritual experience but spiritual beings having a human experience. One need not look outside to find answers. All the answers we seek lie within.

During this journey, I met amazing people from around the world who have accomplished a lot. However, what sets them apart is their mindset. At a personal growth event, I found my tribe of entrepreneurs and change-makers who helped me learn and grow immensely. I was introduced to Consciousness Engineering and new concepts of living.

"If you are always trying to be normal, you will never know how amazing you can be."

Each of us has the responsibility to be the greatest version of ourselves. Some of the things I learned were the distinction between means-goal and end-goal, how to use Creative Visualization to achieve those goals and *Blisscipline* (Discipline of being in the blissful state of Flow). The bridge between the known and unknown - between belief and knowing. Beliefs are the result of our influences (environment, people, books, etc.). It is an external thought or idea which we accept to be good for us. However, we truly know something only when we experience it.

New Models of Reality.

I grew up with many rules & beliefs. Some of them served me well which helped me to grow and some of them did not. It's imperative to distinguish between these. Now I understand that many of these rules were actually my BRULES (Bull Shit Rules) which I discarded later. Some of those BRULES are:

- Religion (A large cult is called a Religion)

- Marriage (a piece of paper which offers social acceptance to a relationship)

- Age (Age is just a number. It's all about our state of mind. There is a difference between being 40 years old and 40 years young - we have a choice! Our body responds to the way we think and we age accordingly.)

- Time (Time is the space between moments. We cherish special moments we experience - these moments could be spread over 3 years or 30 years.)

- University Education (This piece of paper certifies one's academic qualification. The current system focuses on studies, not education.)

Looking back on all the decisions I have made in my life, some of which have had a positive outcome and have helped me to grow and some of which have been negative. When I analyze the basic reason behind each and every decision, these can be narrowed down to two feelings: **Love & Fear**. All the decisions made out of love have lead to positivity and the decisions made out of fear have negatively impacted me. I made a conscious choice thereafter - to only do everything out of love and not because of fear.

Evolution.

All of us are here for a purpose. The end-goal for all of us is to merge with the universal divine consciousness. It is a natural process of evolution. The various stages people evolve, which I believe are:

1. In the first stage, we are the victim - Life happens **TO** us.
2. In the next stage, we are the manifestor - Life happens **BY** us.
3. In the third stage, we are the channel - Life happens **THROUGH** us.
4. In the final stage, we are it and we **MERGE** with the divinity.

In this process, Love is the energy which helps us evolve. There are states of unconditional love starting from the state where we are unable to truly love anyone. The next state is where we start to love ourselves. This is the most important step to start feeling love. Further along, we are able to love a few people unconditionally. The most evolved state is where we feel connected and express unconditional love towards everyone. Very few people are able to reach this stage but we have read of some of these people throughout history. I was fortunate enough to meet one such person - Mother Teresa.

Manifesting My Reality.

We are not our mind. Our mind is just a tool we can use to create anything we want - positive or negative. We are limited only by our thoughts and all of us have the ability to manifest our reality through our thoughts and feelings. I had experienced this earlier on in my life.

Doing something which I was not passionate about was not was not satisfying. What did I really want to do? What would I find purposeful, meaningful and fulfilling which I would enjoy? I realize that I wanted to create and define a new space in India and impact the lives of millions of people with my work. I had no idea how I was going to do either of these.

Entrepreneurship is like jumping off a cliff and figuring out how to build an airplane on the way down.

I got some experience in eCommerce both in India and the US by setting up a sourcing base for gadgets in China and the US and selling in marketplaces in India and the US using drop shipping. This experience in eCommerce helped me immensely when starting my ReCommerce (Reverse Commerce) Venture. This is also what helped me with the initial capital for my venture.

I was influenced by someone in the UK who started his career with ReCommerce of used music records amongst students. He went on to do quite well for himself and also started his own airline. His name is Sir Richard Branson. Elon Musk and his risk taking ability inspired me to think big at the same time.

I've always been fond of using the latest gadgets. I had recently upgraded my phone and was wondering what do I do with my old one. I had a few options:

- Trade it into a local dealer. He would only buy back something if I bought something new from him. Also, the pricing was very inconsistent.

- Use an online classified ad to sell my old phone. I had to list my product and wait for someone to contact me. I wasn't sure whether the callers were genuine buyers, when it would sell or at what price. The experience could be good, bad or ugly.

- Leave it in a drawer somewhere in my house and the device would end up losing value and become dangerous e-waste.

Every problem is an opportunity. Entrepreneurship is essentially about problem-solving.

So I started focusing on this one problem - what do we do with our used gadgets? I did market research, looked at various models around the world, spoke to many different companies. Some of the facts which I came across was astounding:

- India is the world's fastest growing smartphone market at 43% CAGR

- Average replacement period for smartphones is 18 months

- 100 Million smartphones shipped in India in 2015 would come back to the secondary market after 18 months. At an average ASP of US$100, this market is over US$10 Billion and growing rapidly.

- Profit margins on certified pre-owned & refurbished

devices are better than on new ones.

- There are no large organized players in this space currently which is primarily unorganized.

- India has 950 Million mobile phone users and 250 million smartphone users. ReCommerce can be used to bridge this digital divide.

- India is a value and price sensitive market. There is a huge unmet demand for Certified Pre-Owned/Refurbished gadgets from a trusted source with the assurance of a warranty. There is no brand in India currently which has been able to create a mind space among the consumers for these gadgets.

"You never change things by fighting the existing reality. To change something, build a new model that makes the existing model obsolete."

The first step was to provide a consistent, controlled, curated selling experience which was missing. The way e-Commerce was focusing on the buying experience, I wanted to focus on improving the selling experience. The idea was to:

1. Provide an instant price discovery mechanism
2. Free shipment pickup across India
3. Prompt direct payment to the user after verification of the device.

This was an idea worth pursuing. I went about it in an analytical manner the way one goes about building a business:

1. Identify an unsolved problem
2. Find a technologically and logistically viable way to solve

the problem
3. Understand the viability and scalability of the business.

When I connected these three dots was when I started Budli (meaning 'Change' in Hindi). My end-goal was to create and drive change in India. I followed the Lean Startup process - built my POC (Proof of Concept) and MVP (Minimum Viable Product) by initially outsourcing it.

I was just a guy with an idea - no team, finance or partners. I spoke to a few people who questioned my idea, that it had not been done before and if no one else had done it how do you know you will be able to. However, I had a conviction of this being a problem worth solving, and my ability to find a solution to the problem. In life, we regret more of the things we do not do than the things we do. Unless we are prepared to fail, we cannot succeed.

"I don't skate to where the puck is. I skate to where the puck is going."

The initial website was outsourced. I managed to get it up but now how do I validate it? How would I know if users would actually find it useful or not? There was no marketing, no one knew about the website. I started calling up local listings of people interested in selling their devices and asking them to check out the website. One person found it interesting and confirmed the order to sell his device. Awesome! But how do I fulfill the order? I had no logistics partners, no payment mechanism. So I went myself to collect the device and complete the transaction. Initially, I wore many hats - these included tech, marketing, product design, finance, sales, packing and delivery. I was able to resell the device online at a profit and that's how the journey started.

The transactions started growing and I built up a team.

Unfortunately, located in Kolkata, we were facing numerous logistical and tax challenges. I realized that for this venture to grow to its potential, Kolkata wasn't the best place for it. I decided to relocate to Bangalore, set up a team there and scale it up.

The journey is the destination.

It has been an exciting, thrilling and challenging journey. We focused on growing vertically within the categories of Smartphones, Tablets & Laptops. Multiple sourcing, selling channels along with logistics partnerships to cover the entire country were developed. Creating awareness about this space both directly and through partners, we could see a new category emerging.

Using an Omni-Commerce approach converging online and offline, we are able to reach various parts of the country for the sale of refurbished devices under our brand name. The customer is assured that it is a genuine product from a trusted source which having gone through our QC & Refurbishment process, comes with a warranty serviced across India in over 100 locations.

We got recognition for the work we were doing, featured in various national and international media and won numerous awards. The biggest satisfaction personally for me was in seeing the way we started creating an impact on the people and the eco-system around us.

We enable users to sell their devices in a socially and environmentally responsible way and also provide an option to donate the sale proceeds of their device to charity. For every device sold on Budli.in, we ourselves contribute an amount towards a socially impactful cause, creating social change.

"To strive, to seek, to find and not to yield."

During the journey, I've faced numerous challenges. There have been times when I was not sure how I would fulfill the next order. Three things helped me overcome these obstacles:

- Clarity (Being clear about the end-goal)

- Certainty (Knowing that the universe is pushing me forward towards it)

- Purpose (When you walk with purpose, you collide with destiny. Doing something impactful and meaningful. Being part of something greater than ourselves.)

Apart from that above, patience, perseverance and passion are essential as well. I believe that entrepreneurs overcome their problems using these strengths along the way. Sometimes the difference between success and failure is just perseverance.

Over time, every idea, business model, and technology can be copied. The long-term success of any company depends on its vision and core values, which cannot be replicated.

When we start focusing on larger problems, our problems seem so small.

We are living in extraordinary times. Anyone in a remote corner of the world with a smartphone and Internet connection has access to more information than the President of the US had 15 years back.

Technology is radically transforming education, healthcare, financial services & utilities.

The primary medium through which this technology is going to be accessed by millions will be the Smartphone - the catalyst for creating change. ReCommerce has the potential to bridge this digital divide in India between people who have access to technologically advanced devices and those who don't. At the same time, reduce e-waste and help save the environment.

Change is the only constant. I'm manifesting my reality by embracing, creating and driving Budli (change).

Credits:

I am thankful to many people who have helped me in my journey.
Some of the quotes, thoughts and ideas have been inspired by:
William Shakespeare
Alfred, Lord Tennyson
Neale Donald Walsch
Buckminster Fuller
Vishen Lakhiani / A-Fest
Michael Beckwith
Wayne Gretzky
Tony Hsieh
Dr. Peter Diamandis

Rohit Bagaria

Rohit Bagaria is a zentrepreneur and Founder & CVO of Budli.in ('Budli' means Change in Hindi) which is driving change in India through ReCommerce - Reverse Commerce of used gadgets like Smartphones, Tablets & Laptops. Budli.in enables users to resell their used gadgets in a socially and environmentally responsible way and bridges the digital divide between people who have access to technologically advanced gadgets and those who don't. These products are refurbished and sold omni-channel.

He has 15 years of experience in various sectors, including software startup in the Silicon Valley, manufacturing & international B2B sales across 35 countries and eCommerce in India, China & the US. Former Director of Founder Institute (international startup accelerator & launch program) in Kolkata. His education is from UC Berkeley, California & St. Xavier's, Kolkata.

He has won awards like Startup of the Year, Emerging Entrepreneur of the Year, Business Leadership Award and has been featured in various national and international media such as BBC World & Fortune Magazine. He has also been invited to speak at various forums including Indian Institute of Management Bangalore and Calcutta.

Website: www.budli.in
Facebook: https://www.facebook.com/rbagaria
Twitter: https://twitter.com/rohitb
LinkedIn: https://in.linkedin.com/in/rohitbagaria

He has won awards like Startup of the Year, Emerging Entrepreneur of the Year, Business Leadership Award and has been featured in various national and international media such as BBC World & Fortune Magazine. He has also been invited to speak at various forums including Indian Institute of Management Bangalore and Calcutta.

Website: www.budli.in
Facebook: https://www.facebook.com/rbagaria
Twitter: https://twitter.com/rohitb
LinkedIn: https://in.linkedin.com/in/rohitbagaria

5

WHERE KNOWLEDGE FAILS, FAITH TRIUMPHS

- BY DR. MONIKA SINGH

The only survivor of a shipwreck was washed up on a small, uninhabited island. He prayed fervidly for God to rescue him, and every day he scanned the horizon for help, but none seemed forthcoming. Exhausted, he eventually managed to build a little hut out of driftwood to protect him from the elements and in which to store his few possessions.

But then one day, after searching for food, he arrived home to find his little hut going up in flames. The worst had happened; everything had gone in dark coils of smoke. He was stunned with grief, hopelessness and anger. "God, how could you do this to me," he cried. Early the next day, however, he was awakened by the whizzing sound of a ship that was approaching the island. It had come to rescue him.

The disheartened, weary man asked his rescuers: "How did you know I was here?"

They replied: "We saw your smoke signal."

It is easy to get discouraged when things are going bad. But we shouldn't lose heart, because God is at work in our lives, even in the midst of pain and suffering. Remember, the next time your little hut is burning to the ground -- it just may be the smoke signal that summons the grace of God.

Something similar happened to me too. In spite of being a medical doctor, who ought to be guided by science, logic, facts, and experimentation, here is what I have always believed in: FAITH, something that remains the greatest healer.

The year was 2007. Our younger child was in pre-nursery. The older one was in standard 1. Pradeep Chauhan, my doctor husband, developed breathlessness and polyserocitis--a condition in which practically all the membranes of major organs are filled with fluid . Tests revealed typhoid fever and superadded viral infection.. Despite quick, timely treatment, his condition worsened. Further diagnosis revealed that his pericardium, the layer surrounding the heart, was filled with water. The layer that should have been 1mm thick had become 1cm. He had gone wholly bedridden and his condition was progressively deteriorating. We consulted a cardiologist friend. She said that it was due to a severe viral infection, which mostly afflicted children and could turn fatal if further infected by adults. Being a child specialist, my husband had most probably contracted it from his patients Therefore, the only option was to remove the pericardium. However, that would have rendered my husband in a further precarious condition.

I wasn't willing to admit defeat, although my own education and learning hinted otherwise. I had to do something. When I am confronted with a situation that cannot be approached conventionally, I resort to my instinct and faith. I did the same. It was almost that God was holding my hand and guiding me !. Instinctively, my inner voice was guiding me—NOW OR NEVER ! I made a very daring decision. I walked down to a park, 800mts from the hospital. I sat down on a bench. I recollected the turn of events. I remember my husband was advised not to move more than 500 mts at a time. Else, he might collapse! It was 7 am. I called my husband. I told him that he would have to walk to the park to pick me up..else, I am not returning.

The park began to fill with morning walkers. And I waited patiently for my husband. I wasn't sure if he would be able to make it. But in my unwavering faith, I kept on praying. By 9 a.m., the crowd gradually began to shrink.. I had never felt this calm and sure ever in my life before !The situation was : either he would make the 800 meters or collapse within a few steps, causing irreparable damage to himself. And see the God's will and the charisma : by 9.45 a m, I saw my him enter the park. This was the most surreal, faith-building experience I had in my life. I didn't rush to him. I left him behind to find me. He came and sat next to me on the bench. We went home. He chose to take the stairs instead of the elevator. Nobody knew what had happened. Not even the doctors !

This was in August 2007. Slowly and steadily, he started walking and was doing 17 kms every day. By December, he was completely healed. We returned to our cardiologist friend. She did an ECHO. She was amazed to find that the pericardium had returned to its normal size. The water was drained out and the infection was gone. All this, without medical intervention !

The Free Spirit

I am a very intuitive person. I have always been. I have had a mind of my own from a very young age, much to the chagrin of my parents and family. Nevertheless, I have to admit that I come from a family that believes in nurturing the independent spirit, with a sense of due responsibility. My grandfather, late Lal Singh Ji, joined the freedom movement early as a student in Delhi. He fought on the streets for the freedom of India and was jailed innumerable times, where he came into close association with Mahatma Gandhi, Pandit Jawaharlal Nehru, Acharya Narendra Dev, Dr Ram Manohar Lohia, among others. In post-Independence India, he was offered many plum positions which he refused, saying that he would extend full support in the massive task of nation-building as a non-state activist and social worker. He didn't wish to build his political career with high positions of power...He grew up as a revolutionary in the midst of great struggles, perseverance, and fortitude. He told Dr Lohia and Acharya Narendra Dev , who wanted him to join in the post-Independence electoral stream, "Please leave some of us reserved for keeping an eye on how our own rulers behave and conduct the affairs of the state."He quit the Congress and joined the Socialist Party. The formidable group of Socialist leaders, including Jayaprakash Narayan and many other stormy petrels of a disciplined, pro-commoner politics, kept the Nehru regime in leash. If my grandfather could do so much for a beleaguered society, it was because he was truly aided and inspired also by my grandmother, late Sumitra Devi Ji .

My father, Mr Satya Pal Singh, naturally imbibed the spirit of independence and firm conviction. As ordained by his illustrious father, he dutifully took up journalism as his profession, with the idea to utilize the power of pen to help keep some semblance of order in a society full of jerky aberrations. He, together with my mother, Mrs Poonam Singh, a very strong woman, who taught in Kendriya Vidyalay, exerted a great influence on my life. I thank them for nurturing in me the spirit of independence, truthfulness and responsibility in life at a very early stage. Once satisfied with my personal attributes, they allowed me to make my own decisions in every field of life. This unrestricted, disciplined upbringing brought immense strength and grit to my life. And I developed full faith in myself.

My husband, Dr Pradeep Chauhan, too comes from a family that has struggled to make a sound, respectable and purposeful living. On hindsight, I think all these factors shaped our outlook of life and prompted us to move out of our comfort zone when we, as a doctor couple, took a very important, I will call it a unique, decision at a very crucial stage in our career.

Success lies in giving back to society

Ideas such as success and satisfaction may mean different things to different people. In our life, a paradigm shift in our perception of professional success occurred at a point when we were actually highly successful in the traditional sense of the word.

To go back a little in time, Pradeep and I got married early--I during the last year of my medical graduation, before further studies and he while doing his post graduation, first year. After pursuing our further studies and gaining some experience, we started a private practice in Delhi. Shortly afterward, we were running a hospital. In a span of 8 years, we were able to build our moderate medical facility into a highly successful multi-specialty hospital. We were financially well-off and very secure with sufficient recognition within the medical fraternity and in the part of city where we worked. We felt we were at the top of the world. Now when I look back, I think this phase in one's life is when complacency sets in and one's goal in life becomes only wealth accumulation and feeding superficial vanities. Along with financial success and recognition, a sense of ennui also sets in, especially in those individuals who want every aspect of their vision to fructify. We had achieved all that we had wanted, that too quite early in life. 'Where to go from here?' was the million-dollar question that kept tormenting us. We had become like any other doctors, catering to the medical needs of a rich segment of urban population. It was then that my husband had an idea, which I may call great now. We took an impulsive decision. We proposed to make quality healthcare accessible to the 'have-nots' of rural population. We decided to move to a place where there were no hospitals, no qualified medical doctors; where people had to travel long distances for the most basic medical aids. Once resolved to take a plunge, we just shut shop and moved on !.

Today, we are running a multi-specialty hospital at a place, called Chhutmalpur, 45 kms from Dehradun, the capital of Uttarakhand and 25 kms each from Roorkee and Saharanpur. We are offering the best-possible medical services and facilities to the rural masses, at par with those being provided by most reputed hospitals in any Indian city..

The journey, no doubt, was fraught with hurdles. We had to start from the scratch. We erected a moderate structure and moved all our equipment from Delhi to the new premises of hopes and deliveries to the poor, downtrodden sections of society. Somehow, we managed to start our services, including surgeries. We were happy with our mind-boggling initiative and had never thought even in dreams that the worst was yet to come. Our initiative backfired!

The rural folk wouldn't trust us. Possibly, they thought that something was fishy in this whole affair. We were dumb-struck, thinking why the hell we wound up our thriving business in the national Capital, to set up a hospital in a God-forsaken place!! The rural folk thought we had either goofed up big time in Delhi or we had some other vested interest. Rumor-mongering overtook the entire area. Although our resilience level was sky-high and reasonably undiluted, yet we felt flummoxed a little while. Then, God came to our rescue, gave us the courage we needed most . It was Providence that kindled our perseverance and instilled a realization in us that these were simple, uneducated village folks. It was only natural that they viewed our intents with suspicion and with a pinch of salt. So we decided to firmly hold on and focus on making the things work.

We knew that getting qualified doctors to work in our 'rural hospital' was near impossible; we equipped ourselves to manage multiple disciplines. We underwent several training programs, for instance, my husband who was basically trained in Pediatrics, did a course in Orthopedics, while I got certified in Sonography. My husband took care of Orthopedics and Pediatrics, while I managed Gynecology and sinology. Both of us together took care of different aspects of Radiology. For months, we struggled hard, worked round the clock. And then, things gradually began to fall in place.

During this period, our greatest satisfaction came from diagnosing and treating a large number of cardiac patients. Most of these people would have simply died without timely medical aid. Thus, for the first time we got a glimpse of the rural life, how miserably deprived the folks are of even the basic healthcare facilities, something that essentially is within the right of every Indian citizen!

Then something strange happened. We established a rapport with the rural folk. We gained their trust and most importantly their love. News spread about our hospital and the work we were doing. The medical fraternity also came to know about us. Many doctors helped us in different ways. However, the greatest blessing came when highly qualified doctors came and joined our hospital. By now, we had a decent team of about 7 visiting doctors from nearby cities. , So now we are truly a multi-specialty hospital. We found our purpose and meaning in our lives of our profession. It's been 8 years since we started our hospital in this predominantly rural area. There are no regrets and no looking back.

Multi-disciplinary approach in healthcare/Integrated Approach to Healthcare and Healing

In my personal practice, I have evolved a three-pronged approach to treatment. : I integrate faith healing and Indian system of medicine with the conventional Allopathic system, to great advantage of patients

I am studying the Upanishads, the Vedas, and other ancient Indian texts so as to integrate ancient approaches to pregnancy and birthing techniques into my practice.

My first learning from Eastern philosophy is that nature is a bounty of potent medicine , that emotions play a major role in our health, healing energies and emotions , is absolutely safe and is life enhancing. . Western philosophy also nurtured such thoughts. Right in the 15th century, European philosopher and botanist Paracelsus has said, "The art of healing comes from nature, not from the physician. Therefore, the physician must start from nature, with an open mind."

Based on these ancient principles, I am planning to set up spiritual birthing centers all over India, to provide a conducive environment for women to experience the whole journey of pregnancy. I want to hand-hold women right from the first trimester, by activating the chakras, the healing centers of our body and by fostering positive, healthy emotions.

I strongly believe that the human body, just as of every other living creature, is designed to heal itself. As medical practitioners, we have to aid the body in self-healing. Self-healing happens at a very instinctual level. How else would you explain the healing process that occurs in animals after the birthing process? I strongly believe that all humans, animals and creatures actually have the potential to initiate the healing process within themselves. We the humans differ from animals on one count: : we are endowed with emotions. Animals are liberated, for they don't experience emotions to the extent that we do. Improper channeling of emotions is what thwarts the healing process and causes illness. I am able to go beyond medical data and proof of expectant mothers, to tell them to tweak and work on certain areas of their emotions and personality. This feedback has worked wonders for most of them.

For instance, a woman in the seventh month of her pregnancy came to me. Previous consultations and diagnoses revealed that the amniotic fluid in the womb had dried up and would result in stillbirth. To avoid that, an immediate c-section delivery was suggested. I studied the case. I could gather that the lady in question was prone to bouts of prolonged anger. Anger thwarts smooth blood circulation. I admitted her and administered all medical treatments necessary to save the fetus. Simultaneously, I performed chakra healing for 15 days and her womb was once again filled with water because her anger issues were resolved completely. She carried the fetus to term and had a fantastic normal delivery.

The doctor in me and the human being in me are not separate entities. The healing hand is an integral part of my being. It is not just knowledge appended to my personality at a superficial level. It is more a spiritual act. Of course, I don't deny the importance of knowledge and training. However, that alone does not suffice, for it is based on temporary relief/suppression of symptoms. There is no room for healing here. It is not just the physical being that is involved in the healing process. More than that, there are the instinctual, emotional and spiritual dimensions of a human being. I make it a point to encourage my patients and mothers to become inward-looking, to find answers within themselves. A holistic approach to medicine is the need of the hour. Moreover, if one has to achieve that, one has one's own SELF and a whole tradition of Indian medicine and approach to health to fall back on.

Communing with Life

As I have said before, I am an intensely intuitive and spiritual person. Over the years, being so intimately involved with the birthing process, somewhere I developed this very emotional and spiritual connect with newborn babies. I discovered the gift of being able to commune with newborns. To 'commune' is a far deeper and profound level of connecting than what the word 'communicate' connotes. I can understand what is troubling a baby, what the baby wants and so on. There is this fallacious notion that babies are blank in their minds upon being born. However, the fact is that at 6 hours after birth, a baby is at the heights of its consciousness. The baby is actually capable of listening, not just hearing. For instance, it can actually respond to simple instructions. I have recorded videos that show babies responding to simple commands.

This research has paved the way for another idea, which I am trying to experiment and make real. Since the first few years of a child's life are when most development occurs, I have come up with tools for blueprinting the developmental trajectory for babies. I believe that through intervention, virtues of love, compassion, peace, integrity, blissfulness, abundance can be inculcated right from the womb, through the first few hours and days after childbirth. I call this concept, 'Awakening the Womb': Providing the right environment and stimuli to facilitate a holistic development in the womb itself and the hours after birth. These babies are the future of our country. Their health and well-being are so essential. I will soon be publishing a book, detailing my research, experimentation and learning.

Another dimension to communing with life is the doctor-patient relationship. Our attitude to and treatment of patients has to undergo drastic changes. That can happen, that as doctors we are here to do service to those in need. The fact that you are the giving end should only bring in humility. Yes, we have to learn to be objective in our relationship with patients. However, objectivity without compassion and empathy will make one inhuman. So, we must send positive vibes to our patients.

Entrepreneurial Journey

Entrepreneurial spirit came naturally to Dr Pradeep and me. Right after studies, we consciously realized that we are not the stuff to work under someone. This is the first step for any entrepreneur in any field : to have the confidence that you want to and can do something on your own. It was with this confidence and belief that we began our journey.

It took a lot of courage to move out of our comfort zone in Delhi and shift to rural India. To follow your heart and most importantly, to take risks is the hallmark of an entrepreneur.

Most entrepreneurs fail soon after starting a venture because they expect everything on a platter of gold. However, we have learned through long-drawn struggle and lot of pain that all that is a misplaced thinking. Perseverance, despite all odds, is what sustains an entrepreneur in the long run.

Financial sustainability, recognition and an inspiring climate are the key factors to run any business. We all must accept that.. However, an inevitable spiritual satisfaction, is my part of the definition of success which comes only with the knowledge that we have made a difference to people's lives. At some point in time, this awakening must occur in an entrepreneur. This is the message I would like to send to all our budding entrepreneurs.

The entrepreneurial spirit and passion for medicine have been the driving force of our lives. With unflinching faith and strong belief by our side, I know we shall travel very far.

Dr Monika Singh

Dr Monika Singh, M D, Gynaecologist and Obstetrician, who is currently involved in pursuing her 'Miracle Mission Program in Parenting', arose from a farmer's family in western Uttar Pradesh, India. Daughter of a Journalist father, Teacher mother and granddaughter of an eminent freedom fighter, late Shri Lal Singh, who sacrificed his career, wherewithal and comforts of a zamindar family, challenging the might of an alien rule, Dr Monika has always adored her distinguished lineage. As a child, Monika developed unusual patience to sit with her grand-father to listen to the tales of the heroics of freedom fighters and the long-drawn pain and torture they suffered in pursuing their mission of winning freedom for the country.

Thus, an adolescent Monika imbibed the spirit of sacrifice and understood the import of courting pains for the sake of others early in life. When she was eight-year-old, her grand-father once spotted her with other children putting stethoscope on someone's chest, asking her to do deep breathing, so that she could know how healthy her 'patient' was. An overwhelmed septuagenarian lifted her in his lap and blessed, "My child, you are a doctor in making. You have found your way." He added in the same breath : "No noble mission or great work is difficult for anyone to achieve so long as he or she steadfastly pursues the goal with focus, zeal and determination."

Those words of inspiration always rang loud and clear in her mind. As a higher secondary student in Delhi, she realized that a multitude of patients from distant rural areas flocked to big government hospitals like AIIMS, Safdarjung and scores of other facilities, looking for relief either free or at a little cost. Whenever she went to a hospital with her parents for someone's treatment, she felt painfully distressed seeing patients not finding beds in the crowded hospital wards and ultimately lying on the floor. It was then she once told her mother in confidence that if she became a doctor, she would one day set up a hospital in a predominantly rural area to treat sick villagers who lacked resources. Monika's own rural origin, coupled with God's grace for a noble deed, gave her enough strength and courage to firmly set her goal and seriously work on that. Over the years, she became a qualified Gynecologist, Obstetrician, a Sonologist and also a fluent speaker and author.

It is generally conceded that sensitive souls find little or no consolation in their own comforts and luxuries if a greater part of humanity suffers and slogs in conditions of pain. They remain restless and impatient till the time they reach the right spot to relieve the pain of others with whatever resources they command in terms of wherewithal and capabilities. As persons of high integrity and values, they make no compromises, never give in to temptations of lucre, as they stand upright with their sights firmly set on their lofty goals.

It is significant to note that as a student, Monika worked very hard, took special interest in school and college assignments, debates and prominently participated in extra-curricular activities that sufficiently broadened her outlook and gave her strength to face the rigors of life. She possessed a high level of understanding of peer aspirations and matched her personal preferences to form great teams to work in unison and perfect coordination, creating impact on the desired deliveries.

Subsequently, working in Delhi's big hospitals for a couple of years, gave a further push to her burning desire to move closer to those sections of the society that struggled in backwaters, perennially falling into the hands of quacks who played with their lives unmindful of their sinful acts. She worked in AIIMS and Safdarjung Hospital and later on in two large private medical centres to acquire sufficient skills and experience of running hospitals.

At around this time, she met her would-be Paediatrician life partner, Dr Pradeep Chauhan, with similar frame of mind and earnestness, himself hailing from a rural background. Before their marriage was solemnized sometime in February 1998, both of them decided to prepare themselves to serve the rural folks who neither had any medical facilities available locally, nor enough money to travel to big cities for the treatment of their patients.

With their moderate means at hand, they set up a private hospital in a West Delhi colony and ran it independently for five years. Their 40-bedded hospital was working wonderfully well, where they had made special arrangement for treatment of the poor and the hapless patients. This doctor duo, however, had a deep pain lurking somewhere in their hearts--the targeted rural mission looked prominently amiss on their scoreboard. So, one fine morning, they set out to a rural area falling between Roorkee and

Dehradun and spotted a location to fulfill their dreams. In about two years time, a 50-bed, multi-specialty, 24-hour emergency hospital, named Ayushman Hospital and Trauma Centre, came up at a little known, mofussil place, called Chhutmalpur, to the pleasure of the locals, whose sick had gasped for a breath all these years.

It is noteworthy that between Roorkee, Saharanpur and Dehradun, this hospital serves as a major medical lifeline today for the locals, especially the villagers. Since the hospital is located on the highway, those travelling between these cities, in the midst of heavy traffic, find the facility providing them immense sense of safety and security. This hospital, thus, remains a boon for this area, conducting free OPDs on designated days for poor patients and provides them plenty of special concessions on other hospital expenses.

However, Dr Monika's goal far exceeds her present achievements. Simultaneously, she has embarked upon a 'Miracle Mission Program', where her purpose as a Gynaecologist and Obstetrician is to serve as a Catalyst in Spiritual Birthing. She proposes to help start 100 Spiritual Birthing Centres by 2025, to help unleash the power that parents possess and help them discover their most effective parenting tools in their own parenting style. With her conviction that a great person is a father or a mother who makes sacrifices to do whatever is the best for their children, so that they become ideal citizens, Dr Monika has taken up this 'Miracle Mission Program'. This emerges from her realization that children are not only the parents' future, but also the future of their country.

Dr Monika, a mother herself, blessed with two children, developed over the years, a keen interest in the behaviors of the newborn kids. She initiated an intensive research in this field and found out how mental conditioning & belief systems of parents and families affect the outcome of pregnancies and conditions of the newborn babies. As these babies grow up into toddlers, nursery goers, to the time they reach early junior schools, the programming & conditioning of their subconscious minds is done up to 98% and more. Their entire life runs and re-runs on these early unconscious & carefree programming patterns of mental conditioning, resulting in some kind of a butterfly effect in their lives.

With the purpose of spreading this awareness by educating the young parents, would-be parents and helping their young ones to bloom, Dr Monika regularly organizes parenting programs. Beside her hospital duties, she remains actively involved in holding events and camps, spreading awareness on the subject that goes by the name of 'Power Parenting Program', a blueprint to successful parenthood.

6

THE RISE OF THE PHOENIX

- BY SADANANDA MURTHY, FOUNDER OF SUSHMA INDUSTRIES

The rise of the Phoenix.

A pioneer is one who perceives an opportunity where, apparently, none exists. I say this from my own experience. Way back in 1986, when I ventured into business, I had perceived a lacuna in the Indian industrial environment. There was a dearth of affordable testing, measuring and calibration equipment/instruments. As a result, Indian products in the electronics and mechanical industries fell short of overseas products in terms of quality and precision.

Indian manufacturers were at a disadvantage for two reasons -- one, imported products were very expensive; second, while, manufacturers in other countries invested about 3-4% of their revenue on procuring and using testing and measuring instruments, Indian entrepreneurs invested a meager 0.01%. For instance, major automotive manufacturers and electrical industries in India invested heavily in production but little on quality control. Hence, India lost out to imports and failed to export indigenous products. This was one of the primary reasons why our GDP had dipped by several folds in the 80s.

Therefore, I took advantage of this gap in the market. I took it up as a challenge. Suddenly it became clear. My motto was to design, develop and manufacture affordable solutions of the highest quality for testing, measuring and calibration and thus came into existence Sushma Industries, started along with the greatest support of my wife A.S.Meenakshi. My business is a coalition of precision engineering and mechanical engineering. We started as a manufacturer of slip rings, load cells, torque sensors, tool kits etc. and upgraded to torque, force and pressure test, measurement and calibration systems. Later I also established a calibration laboratory offering calibration services to prove the quality of our products in-house to customers in various areas such as torque, force, pressure, mass, volume, density etc.

The initial years were not easy. However, this is true of any business enterprise, more so in the manufacturing segment. In my case, the resistance was compounded by the fact that the products were absolutely new and fresh in the Indian market, although there were plenty of imported products. Anything new is initially met with resistance. We had to break the barriers. Customers weren't willing to try our products. The foremost reason being that I was a local manufacturer. Besides, we had no brand identity, let alone brand loyalty. Start-ups with low capital such as mine, cannot even think of investing in advertising. Customers would rather go for imported equipment than try my products before deciding on its quality and efficacy. I wasn't even allowed to enter the premises of several industries when I went over to introduce and market my products. I persisted because I knew the quality and potential of my products. Such a pity, that an Indian had to prove to his own countrymen that his products can be better than imported products!

It was the TATA group or then called Telco's R&D team that first gave us a chance. Reaching out to Telco was also not easy. It took several visits and consistent follow-up. I was bent on making an entry somewhere. That was a turning point. Soon Sushma's credibility increased and other industries such as Pricol, Bajaj, ARAI, ISRO, BARC, etc. bought and implemented our products. Our USP was that we offered SOLUTIONS by customizing and manufacturing the products for their requirement, then providing technical support to help them use the product effectively. The other big advantage was of course the products came at a far lesser price than the imported ones. If another country charged Rs.10 lakh to install their product, we could do the same, mind you, without compromising on quality at Rs.3 lakh. The value we provided through our service was the deal clincher rather than price. Our products, therefore, were substituting imports. Over time the customers saw high value in our offering and had even advised us to increase our prices so we had more funds to invest and grow. That was a big achievement in itself in the 80s when the attraction towards imports was very high and there was really no conducive ecosystem to talk of for startups. The last 10-15 years have really seen the spurt of an ecosystem that is very, very start-up friendly.

Torque Man of India

Gradually, the number of players in this market segment increased. I wanted to do something unique. I always looked for challenges. Otherwise, business becomes static; there is no scope for growth and evolution. You have to realign your goals because the environment around you is always in a flux. That's when I took up the challenge of manufacturing technically complex highly niche equipment to measure torque. Many in the industry had tried their hand at this solution and had failed. By god's grace, I was able to manufacture many such equipment as customized products and as standard product offering. Customers began knocking on our doors to find solutions for their Torque measurement challenges. Since then, I have been called by our customers as the 'Torque Man of India'. Today, we have a wide array of products to test Torque and Force.

At Sushma, we don't believe in just selling a product. We believe in giving customers a package that includes the product, the technical know-how to use it and more importantly why and how the product is important in the specific application or context, or the implication of a faulty mechanical condition. For instance, the consequences of a bolt not tightened sufficiently or of a spring whose functioning is not tested properly in a gun. **I always say that we don't offer products but we provide solutions.**

Temple for Calibration

In the year 1995, Sushma achieved a unique milestone. I had by now indigenously designed, developed and manufactured over 100 products. I was now focused on increasing my customer base and penetrating more number of markets. But, how do I convince potential customers that my products are as good as imported ones? So, the next logical challenge was that I needed to create an evaluation system and process to test my own products and certify their quality. So I created a framework of requirements and criterion, against which to test my products so they would carry a genuine tag of credibility in the market. We launched the Sushma Calibration and Testing Facility as per IS/ISO 17025 adhering to stringent National and International standards. Our facility received the National Accreditation Board for Testing and Calibration

Laboratories (NABL) accreditation in 2002. We thus became the first Calibration Laboratory in India for torque and force! I call it 'the temple for calibration', with a singular focus on serving customer need for high precision. You may call me a perfectionist. But I believe that whatever you do, you have to do it with passion and dedication.

Since the laboratory was one of a kind in India, the name of the calibration laboratory grew very fast, since customers who had imported products could also get their products regularly validated to keep up with the traceability requirements in a quick time vs sending it out of the country for expensive and long lead time calibrations. Even today our Torque laboratory has the highest capacity in South-East Asia.

As many laboratories flourished in the market and technology advanced, there was a need for a thorough criteria required in the market to define the quality of Calibration and testing Laboratories. Few years ago, I was invited by NABL to create that SPECIFIC CRITERIA on which the laboratories can prepare for the NABL audits, and NABL had a more scientific way of awarding technical results. I helped create a set of 450 page criteria along with the support of my wife, which every Calibration and Testing Laboratory should follow. Incidentally, these accreditation criteria are followed all over Asia.

You see, my beginnings were very humble. I have come up the hard way. I have faced competition at every level. My education was not a smooth process. When I was in class 7, the concept of high school had just been introduced(previously high school was considered after class 8 for three years). This had a big impact where there was a huge rush with double the students for joining the new high school. I had to leave my home town and come to Bangalore for my high school. By the time I completed pre-university at St. Joseph's College, Bangalore, my passion for electronics engineering had blossomed. Once again, during my engineering days electronics was in great demand and there were just a couple of colleges offering the course. Although I did not get a seat in Bangalore, I got admission for a B.Tech-Electronics course in the Regional College in Mysore. This course was offered as collaboration with the American government. To my misfortune, the course was canceled midway. The government was obliged to absorb us into the engineering course. The only option offered was the mechanical stream Or I had to quit entirely.

After graduation, I worked for an electronics company for a year. Due to family circumstances, I had to quit the job and I ventured into entrepreneurship to support my brother who was going through a professional crisis. I was with my brother for about a decade and then I ventured out alone in 1985.

The year of turmoil and resurrection

"Difficulties strengthen the mind, as labor does the body."
            – Seneca, Roman philosopher.

The myth of the Phoenix rising out of its ashes is no unfamiliar story and is a perfect metaphor for my life. I have gone through several hardships. But to know that I have survived sends a shiver down my spine. And my family, especially my wife has been the one constant in my life who has been responsible for my rebirth as it were.

Words like turmoil and resurrection are applicable not only to larger than life mythical heroes and their journeys transcending time and space; rather to the ordinary human being, and his humble journey through life.

The year 1985 was the lowest point of my life. I had been married for 4 years, and had my daughter who was just 3years old. In pursuit of helping others, I had hurt myself emotionally, financially and professionally. I was literally broke and had loans to repay. I was depressed. To compound the problem, I met with an accident and was confined to my home for over 3 months. During this phase, my wife Meenakshi and my relatives especially BR Nataraju supported me tremendously. My wife has stood by me through thick and thin. This help reposed my faith in human goodness. Their support and strengthening myself physically and emotionally through yoga practice helped me tide over this difficult phase.

We lived in a small house and I worked in our kitchen, manufacturing. Once I got the order from Kirloskar my business began to look up. But soon that dream crashed within a few months. But later the same year I built a factory and business took off in full swing. We delight in the beauty of the butterfly, but rarely admit the changes it has gone through to achieve that beauty.

But this decision to go solo, in hindsight was the best decision of my life. Entrepreneurship is a very exciting journey. It gives you the adrenalin rush experience every now and then. Of course, you cannot get carried away. You have to tread very cautiously and take calculated risks.

I am very passionate about designing instruments and machines. I thoroughly enjoy this creative process; a culmination of varied skills, areas of knowledge and experience. Building customized products to fulfill specialized needs gives me great pleasure. Customization helps me think better, and create newer solutions. It is a way of being in touch with the new tidings in the industry. Whatever be the nature of the product, I design keeping the user experience in mind. This is also a standard brief that I give to my R&D team. Although our products are highly technical and sophisticated, we work towards making the interface user-friendly and most importantly adds value to their work.

Building Enduring Relationships in a value-driven enterprise

The one person who laid the foundation for the values and principles of which I am integral to my personal and professional life, is S. R. Rama Murthy, my high school English teacher in Srirampuram, Bangalore. He would walk me to his house and give me lessons in culture and ethics.

My good fortune is that many people have walked hand in hand with me during my journey. I have always valued human relationships, of whatever nature they may be. My employees are my greatest assets. When I started my factory, two youngsters worked for me. Along with my wife and me, they worked from 9 am to 10 pm for 7 long years. I am greatly indebted to them. The first residential lands I bought and built a home, I registered in their names. Winston Churchill has said, "We make a living by what we get. We make a life by what we give." I am keenly interested in the upliftment of the people who work for me.

At work, we live the attitude 'Everything is possible'. Because, if I hadn't said that to myself, I wouldn't be where I am today. We understand that every individual has his own potential and hence we provide a co-operative environment for mutual growth and learning. We support them to dream big and yet be grounded in reality. I have always promoted a culture of joy and happiness among my employees. We empower people to lead a balanced life and encourage them to take up responsibilities. I am concerned about the physical and mental well-being of my employees. We started as a family of four and we have now grown into a family of 65. This strong family culture is the highlight of our organization.

I have never given into instant gratification, either in relationships or in success. I focus on long-term goals and enduring relationships. I put in a lot of effort to build relationships. Many of my past customers are also my good friends. Which is why, at Sushma, we honor commitment to every customer requirement. We earnestly maintain confidentiality in terms of customer applications and the products we design and develop. *Ease of doing business with us makes quality a part of work culture. Else, quality assurance becomes an arduous and painful task.

My greatest motivation is that the products I build facilitate other entrepreneurs to manufacture and sell high-quality products. I look at them as stakeholders in my business and hence I am responsible for customer satisfaction.

I recollect, in the early days of my entrepreneurship, my reputed auditor B.S. Shivanna had asked me, "Do you want to make money or do you want to enjoy building a business professionally?" Without a second thought, I had answered, "Of course, I want to first and foremost enjoy my entrepreneurship life." My agenda is to do business ethically. Entrepreneurship has provided me the space to do businesses, on my own terms; I am a strong believer in the value-based system of doing business.

Currently, I am building a large calibration machine that costs about 10 crores abroad. My machine costs only about 4 crore. I have always believed in designing and offering affordable solutions because moneymaking is not the primary agenda of my life. Pursue your passion with hard work and dedication, success and money will follow.

Entrepreneurial Qualities

If I have to look back and identify the qualities that have led me to where I am today, they are:

- I am a self-starter. My product line proves it. I am highly motivated. When an idea hits me, I see it through to its execution. Nothing can stop me.

- Dedicated Effort, Concentration, Perseverance, because you cannot taste success easily or early. It takes its own course and time. I confess with pride that I have failed over 10 times before I could come up with a good solution or product.
- Mental strength, grit and courage to tackle and overcome what may appear to be insurmountable obstacles.
- Co-operation is another main ingredient. None can achieve their goal without co-operation of all stake holders who are all human beings. It is all about the confidence in building successful relationship with all people from employees, partners, vendors, statutory, funding agencies, customers ,etc.
- Approaching the relation building out of love and care makes all the difference. We handle 20% machines/systems/technical matters and 80% humans.
- Positive outlook because just when you take two steps forward, for no fault of yours, you may retreat by four steps. But you have to just go on. You cannot give up.
- Constant innovation in any business is the sure shot way of remaining competitive in the global marketplace. Imagination and creativity are the driving force for innovation.
- Adaptability to change is a quality I imbibed over the years. If you resist change, be it in market requirement, your own method of functioning, you will make it difficult for yourself. A flexible mental makeup and working environment are essential.

The future is very promising for Sushma Industries. We are in the process of building many new technologies and products - Wireless Sensing, Smart Sensors, new Sensing technologies, Automation, Robotics and Nuclear Energy, Renewable Energy to name a few. We aim to expand our presence across many more industrial sectors and across countries. I want Sushma to be known as a brand that offers products and services not just on par with international standards but which creates new benchmarks globally; as an organization that offers a holistic and fulfilling career opportunity and environment; as an organization that operates on the highest ethical plane.

Sushma Industries is now under the able leadership of Suveer Sadanand, my son. I am happy that Sushma is now in the hands of a second-generation entrepreneur. Initially, he was, like every youngster of his time, contemplating to be a motorsport racer or explore opportunities to start a new venture in India. But he soon began to realize the immense potential of our business if infused with new blood. He understood the impact of the solutions on our customers' business. He felt that about 4 decades of hard work and an enormous product line had barely reached a sizeable market. He decided that he would join the business and make sure it grows manifold. He is working towards a 10-fold growth over 5years. In the last three years, he has been successful in achieving a three-fold growth.

With more time to spare, I have now donned the cap of a mentor, advisor, and trainer. But learning is a life-long process. Books and observation are my mainstays for learning. I am a keen observer of human interactions and behavior. In fact, when I am on vacation, I observe people or I read books.

Many business associates seek advice. I am happy to share my experiences and insights. Knowledge is meant to be disseminated. I am happy if I can help in somebody else's success. In an official capacity as General Secretary of Metrology Society of India- an initiative to spread the importance of measurements/metrology, I have been instrumental in training and testing about 600 people in calibration science whereby improving the quality of production of industries, Calibration and Testing Labs from India, Srilanka, UAE, Saudi Arabia, etc. with the support of Government agencies. We have trained many people from Toyota, TVS group, Mahindra, Bajaj, Tata, ISRO,DRDO, BHEL among others on how to measure and maintain quality requirements for their products.

Experience is the best teacher. If I have to share my learning with budding entrepreneurs, then here are some pointers:

- Don't work only to make money. As Henry Ford, Founder, Ford Motor Company, has said, 'A business that makes nothing but money is a poor kind of business'. Profitability is important to sustain and grow your business. But, at all times integrity and human values must be prioritized.
- Entrepreneurship requires passion. If you can't enjoy what you are doing, you may not last long.
- Conviction in yourself and your capabilities is very essential. Confidence in yourself and pride in your business is essential.
- Practice an optimistic approach to human interaction. Give feedback, not criticism. Do not find fault, but focus on finding remedies.
- Think out of the box. Be innovative in your approach to problem solving.
- Train your mind to convert every hardship into an opportunity.

Just as my generation was, so is the next generation at risk of compromising on the quality of life. The only things that I was taught to bother about, during my growing up years, were studies, working and making money to feed the family. I wish we were also told about how to lead a quality, stress-free life with peace of mind while accomplishing our dreams and goals facing the challenges in good stead. Most of us are not even aware that eventually quality of life is the most important asset. As parents and mentors, I strongly feel that we should inculcate quality of life as the most important experience that children should work towards.

Sadananda Murthy

An entrepreneur and knowledge philanthropist, Mr. R. Sadananda Murthy, is well known for being a major catalyst in improving the Testing and Calibration Industry of India for 45 years. He is also popular among family and friends for being a guide. He ignites young minds to dream big and helps them create a beautiful vision for the future.

Mr. R. Sadananda Murthy, born in 1951, in a village near Tumkur, Karnataka, began his journey with humble beginnings. Being born to a primary school teacher and a home maker, fighting odds and working hard for growth became a habit. Post his education in Mechanical Engineering and a post graduate Diploma in Production Management, he went on to work with a company in the measurement industry.

He founded Sushma Industries in 1986 along with his wife

A.S.Meenakshi. In the past three decades, Sushma has become a major brand in India in the Measurement, Testing and Calibration Industry. Today Sushma Industries Pvt. Ltd. provides Torque, Force, Pressure Measurement and Test Systems and Solutions with over 200 products for over 30 different industry sectors. With a philosophy of providing solutions instead of just products has helped more than 4500 customers reap profits. These products are used in R & D teams, quality control departments or end of line testing in production line or in dedicated Testing or Calibration Laboratories.

Forty-five years of experience in the field of metrology has moved his focus to create a better quality or Metrology Infrastructure in the country which will play a major role in the growth of the manufacturing industry. His energy and intention to give back to the industry has been well appreciated by being one of the technical experts of NABL Committee and a Chairperson for Specific Criteria-Mechanical calibration group. These specific criteria are followed in the country as a laboratory technical standards and guides.

Mr.Murthy has two children: daughter, Sushma and son, Suveer.

Education

B Tech-Ed. in Mechanical Engineering Degree in 1971 from Regional College of Education

Post Graduate Diploma in Production Management in 1972 from St.Josephs College, Bangalore

Professional:

He is also the general secretary of Metrology Society of India-Southern Region (MSI-SR). He has a great vision to bring together scientific, industrial, legal metrologists and service providers like calibration/testing labs, certifying and accreditation bodies under one roof so that, quality products and globally acceptable results are produced and uniformity in measurement is achieved throughout the country which in turn will help the economic growth of India.

Mr. Murthy also represents the industry in Bureau of Indian Standard (BIS) to help evaluate and introduce many new standards in the field of testing and calibration for India.

Connect with me

Email: rsada.murthy@sushmaindustries.com
Website: www.sushmaindustries.com
LinkedIn: www.linkedin.com/rsadamurthy
Facebook: www.facebook.com/rsada.murthy

7

CRAFTING DREAMS

- BY BHAKTI SANGHAVI, ENTREPRENEUR, EVENT MANAGER, PHILANTHROPIST

When you ask a child at the age of 4, where do you want to go? The child responds pointing at the sky – "I want to go to the moon, I want to be in the sky, I want to go on the clouds." Few years later, when you ask the child at the age of 8, where do you want to go? The child responds – "I want to go to New York, I want to go to London, I want to go to Paris." As the child grows into his/her teens and you ask the same child at the age of 15, where do you want to go? The child responds – "I want to go to Singapore, Malaysia, Dubai." At the age of 20, reality sets in and you ask the grown up adult, where do you want to go? The adult replies – "Bangalore, Mumbai, Delhi, Hyderabad!" and few years later, the life of this adult just becomes about going from home to office and back home again.

For most people, the ability to dream shrinks as they grow old. And the beauty is that their mind justifies it as 'learning from experience'. For me, personally I disagree that these people are learning. I feel learning is to understand why one failed and to better themselves to conquer that failure and emerge victorious. I believe that life is a gift and each one of us owes it to our creator to dream big and live those dreams. It is our responsibility to dream and achieve!

My story is that of a girl born and brought up in a middle class Gujrati family, seen through financial crisis yet believed in myself to dream and achieve!

Crisis seeds mediocrity

Being the youngest of three children, I was the most pampered at home. My sister describes me as a bully. I would cry on the birthday of my siblings because I would want to receive the birthday bumps as well even if it was not my birthday. Academically I was bright and would always make my parents proud through my schooling days. I led a pretty normal and happy life as a child till one day tragedy struck.

My father who was a traditional Gujrati businessman having a retail store one day received a threat call from a mafia goon in Bangalore to vacate the store premises. There was no reasoning to the demands placed on my father. Suddenly the environment at home was filled in fear. I was in my 8th grade and overnight we had to leave home, stop going to school and had to leave the city for our safety. For the next two months, living in my relatives home in Mumbai, I saw my father deal with this uncalled for crisis without the support of anybody.

Seeing my father helpless against people with power seeded a deep hatred within me against the mighty and the rich. Every single day of those two months we lived in the fear of losing our father, we prayed for mercy and all we wanted was a normal life. Those sixty days of living away from our own home and school put me in a shell as a child. The crisis got resolved with my father seeding to the demands and letting go of his retail store – our only source of bread.

My father is a fighter and a true inspiration for me. Even after losing everything he had created, he did not lose hope. He worked hard to make ends meet. Though our life was not back on track as it was before, we at least had the resources to meet our bare necessities. Looking back, I realise that the biggest impact of this crisis we experienced as a family was not the loss of wealth, but the loss of faith and belief. The way we looked at money as a family had changed. We lived with a mind-set of scarcity and fear. Our dreams had shrunk!

As I grew into my teens and entered college, the concept of money created fear in my mind. I got an admission into one of the best colleges in the country – Mount Carmel College. I pursued my graduation in Commerce. Every girl around me in college had aspirations. They spoke about dreams and careers and somehow I never had anything to say when these conversations came up. My mind would go blank. I had lost the ability to even think and dream of a future and that was completely normal and acceptable for me. Crisis had successfully seeded mediocrity and scarcity in my mind and I was not even aware of it.

The Awakening

I met my now husband – Rajiv Talreja through a common friend during my college days. We started off as good friends. He once invited me to a weekend workshop and said that it would be a great experience. I went for the program only because I did not know how to say no to Rajiv. The weekend was life transforming. There were about 100 college students like me but the workshop had nothing to do with our academics or career. The workshop was about life, emotions, relationships and beliefs. The weekend shattered my limitations and gave me the awareness that I had locked my mind with a whole set of fears and doubts. I had even forgotten how to breathe with freedom and for the first time in 8 years I felt like I could control my own life and my own feelings.

I was so impacted by the weekend that I decided to join as a volunteer intern into the youth organization which hosted this program. This internship was a defining experience in my life. As a part of my internship I promoted the monthly workshop to impact the lives of more students. Within 3 months thanks to my performance as an intern, I grew in the organization and became a part of the core team of the organization. We were 6 of us on the core team including the Founder of the organization. We were leading the organization with a mission to make it India's #1 Youth Organization.

I completed my graduation and decided to join the youth organization full time. From one city, we scaled the organization to 3 cities and impacted over 5,000 students through our transformation programs. Suddenly the way I saw myself had changed. I believed that I could dream and achieve. My family never really objected to me working barring a few times when my father would suddenly slip into being a traditional controlling parent. Every time he resisted, my resolve became stronger. From a cynic, I had transformed to living in a world of idealism. Nothing was impossible according to me. The more I was told to not trust people easily, the more I trusted people easily. The more I was told to play safe and think small, the bigger my dreams became. All that I dreamt of was to make our youth organization the biggest and the best youth organization and to change the lives of the youth of

India.

The Dejection

Success can be distracting. This was a lesson I was fortunate to learn quite early in my life. Our organization grew very fast, but not necessarily strong. The core team that had seen the organization through its golden period started disintegrating. Individuals started moving on to pursue their personal career goals of entrepreneurship, higher studies and corporate jobs. I considered myself as a loyalist. For me building this youth organization was a mission till one day in a coffee shop meet.

I was presenting the finances of the organization to the new core team at a coffee shop. There was a proposal floated by the founder to make some investments in his personal education for attending some international courses. The finances of the organization did not look in great shape so I expressed my views about the timings of his investment. The core team backed my rationale and rejected the idea of making the learning investments at that point and suddenly the founder was the only voice backing his own proposal. This did not go down well with him and he looked in my eye and said, "This is my organization, this is my money and you are nobody to tell me what I should do with my money."

For me, this was a shocker. Here was a person whom I considered as my mentor, my guru, who had changed my life, taught me how to believe in myself, how to stand up and do what's right; today telling me that I do not have a right to have a voice. In that one moment, everything shifted for me. I was shattered and shaken up. I decided this was my last day working there and I left in absolute dejection.

From Fear to Faith

Moving on from the youth organization was not easy for me. It was clear that it was the right thing to do but not at all an easy thing to do. This was the time I had to dig within and ask myself, what makes me happy? What do I love doing? There was also a lot of fear within which clouded my thoughts. Suddenly the feeling of being orphaned set in and I started questioning everything I had learnt during my days at the youth organization. The cynic within wanted to kick-in and that's when I started asking myself the real questions of who am I and who do I want to be as a person?

I learnt the most valuable lesson of distinguishing between the message and the messenger. Somewhere I had lost my own power because I made somebody else the hero in my life. The moment I realized this, I regained myself and grounded myself in the power of my learning and teachings I had at the youth organization. My hurt healed and turned into gratitude because I knew something bigger and better was waiting. I chose faith over fear and decided to start up. I chose trust over dejection and I decided to create an organization that would represent trust, care and creativity.

Choosing to move forward rather than stay stuck in a drama of emotions, dejection and blame was the best decision I made. Looking back today, my belief on – 'God always has a plan' just gets stronger. If that coffee shop meeting would not have happened, I would probably have gotten lost in the shadow of somebody else. I would never have explored my own dreams, my own creation.

Taking the center stage

March 2007, I laid the foundation of a new dream. I started Center Stage – an event management company along with a good friend of mine as the co-founder. We had no idea about events but we were clear we wanted to create wonderful memories for our clients by creating an experience rather than an event.

Our first event was for a large corporation who wanted their office decorated to mark the beginning of the new financial year. All we had to do was put up about 1,500 balloons. Our level of ignorance about events was so high that we did not even know that you can get vendors who have inflators to blow the balloons. We actually took the help of a few friends and blew all the balloons by ourselves and went and put it up in the client's office. While the highlight of this experience was the level of inexperience and ignorance we had, it also is a personal highlight for me on our commitment and how far we have come.

The next 3 years was about taking baby steps to give Center Stage an identity in the event management space. We never said no to any kind of work. We did birthday parties, corporate conferences, weddings, anniversary parties and any and all type of events. Looking back I believe this was a mistake because we wanted to be everything to everybody and ended up being nobody.

We made all the mistakes a start-up would make – be it under-pricing ourselves, not building a niche for ourselves, over-hiring. But one thing which was a factor of pride for me throughout this journey was that we never ever let our clients down. We never ever breached a promise to a client. We never compromised on our delivery to the client.

Letting go to letting grow

In the 3rd year of our journey as Center Stage, we decided to take a big leap and host our own event for the public at large. We conceptualized a stand-up comedy show and decided to bring down the top comedians of India including the likes of Kapil Sharma, Bharti Singh, Krushna and Sudesh on to one stage for a 2 hour program. This was a big step we were taking to put our brand in the spotlight across the city.

We scheduled the program for the 9th January 2011 and gave ourselves a good 5 months to pull it off. We divided our responsibilities and went all out to make it happen. We knew right from the start that the success of the event was twofold. Firstly to ensure a full house and secondly to have enough sponsors to break even on the costs of the event. Two months before the event suddenly I had a lot of the clients my business partner was handling raising concerns about the quality and timely delivery of our work to them. When confronted, my business partner justified with all the work she was doing for our upcoming mega event. Though unacceptable, I decided to move on.

Less than 20 days to the mega event when we sat for a joint review, we realized that there was no progress on the deliverables of my business partner. For me this was a breach of trust which shook my foundation of our partnership. We decided to move on and take charge but with every passing day leading to the mega event, the deficit in trust only grew. My initiative grew and my business partner's inaction towards the event grew.

Two days ahead of the event, we knew the program was going to be a full house based on our ticket sales; however we had no sponsors, which meant that we were going to have to pay out of our own pockets to cover up the losses. I was mentally prepared because we had to own up for our inefficiency. At 11pm, my partner walked up to me and said I think we should cancel the event because it makes no sense to do an event making massive losses. I was very clear that were not going to send 2,000+ people who had trusted us and purchased the tickets back because we had not done something well at our end. I stuck to my decision and did not budge because I knew that this loss is a lesson for us to learn and cancelling the event is equivalent to surrendering to the internal inefficiency and breaking a promise to the public.

The big day came. The event was super hit. The celebrities were in awe of the flawlessness of our work. We were overwhelmed with praise and appreciation from all corners. While I was happy with what we had pulled off, at the back of my mind, the misalignment with my business partner who was my dearest friend was a cause of worry.

One week after the completion of the event, when the two of us sat down; there was a sense of hurt and disappointment both of us had towards each other. I was unhappy with her responsiveness through the journey over the last 5 months and she was unhappy with my decision to go ahead with the event even though we knew we were making the losses. The understanding that our aspirations for the organization and our styles of working are completely different was a big point of realization. We knew that even if we moved forward, we would constantly battle this disconnect at work.

The friendship meant most to the two of us and we realized that we were better friends than business partners and probably that was the precise reason that Center Stage had never really taken off. Looking back, this was a great decision for the both of us. I am a believer that for a business to achieve success, there has to be absolute synchronization of energies within. And when the energies of the people at the helm of a business differ, then the business revolves around at a certain level forever. Because we were more friends than business partners, we would always draw a line in the amount we would challenge and push each other.

The moment had come for us to take a call on how we wanted to part ways. We had two options, one of us takes Center Stage forward and the other steps out, we shut Center Stage and both of us start afresh individually. Option two was not an option for both of us because deep down inside we did not want the name of Center Stage to fade away. At this point, this was a big bone of contention between the two of us on who would take Center Stage forward. We had scheduled a meeting time and date to discuss this along with a few good friends who came forward to help us arrive at a decision. I was extremely nervous because I wanted to take Center Stage forward and yet did not want any kind of bitterness in our relationship.

At that moment, a conversation with my now husband, then good friend Rajiv helped me get clear of what was more important to me. I decided I would give my business partner the option to choose whatever she wanted and I was prepared that I will let go of my brain child Center Stage to give myself a fresh start with a fresh ideology. This was not an easy decision for me to take. But I took it because I felt by doing so I no longer give any reason from my side for our relationship to go bitter and I give myself a new challenge to build something from scratch and build something that can stand for what I stand for.

The mission to craft dreams

For me this was a fresh life, a fresh start; like a blank canvass where I could create the deepest desires of my heart. The name DreamCraft came up when Rajiv asked me the question, 'What do you want this business to do?' And without a second thought I answered saying – "I want to build a workplace that will fulfil the dreams of people. I want to build a business which is like a genie to anyone it comes in contact with, be it our clients, our team members or my own dreams." On 3rd February 2011, I started my second venture – DreamCraft Events and Entertainment.

Thanks to all the lessons I had learnt in Center Stage, I made the corrections. I was very clear that DreamCraft will not be a 'Do everything for everybody' company. I knew that DreamCraft has to be an exclusive corporate events company because there was also a massive gap in the industry for professionally and ethically run event management companies which could deliver high quality services with value for money for the clients. We started DreamCraft with a 3 member team and in the first year of DreamCraft we did 3 times the highest turnover I had ever done in the 4 years of Center Stage. I knew this was a sign that we were doing things right.

One of my big personal dreams was to gift my wedding to my parents and not burden them with the expenses of my big fat wedding. I was also very clear that I wanted a big fat Indian wedding for myself as a reward for the years of work we had put in. On 30th November 2012, I got married to my long time friend and business partner – Rajiv Talreja and both of us funded a big fat Indian wedding out of our personal income from DreamCraft as a gift to our parents.

For us the dreams got bigger once we did this for ourselves. We wanted to make sure we crafted the dreams for our team members as well. For the last 4 years in DreamCraft, every team member lists out their dreams and we as a team work together to ensure that the business grows consistently to be able to fund the dreams of our teams. Be it funding their own marriage, to supporting the further education of their siblings and children or to take travel breaks with their families – as a company we ensure the dreams of every team member are taken care of. This has allowed me to build a highly committed and competent team. My team is my pride today and fulfilling their dreams is my purpose.

Because we have such a simple purpose of crafting dreams for everyone, the commitment levels and standard of events we deliver for our clients is way above expectations of our clients. We take pride in boasting that a client who starts working with us, never leaves us. Delivering value and keeping our word is the most fundamental thing for us at DreamCraft.

In a short span of time, DreamCraft has achieved a lot of milestones and made a mark as an industry leading Event Management Company. From being official event partners to some of the most prestigious events like the International Spelling Bee Championship, National Achievers Conference, the Global IUAI Conference which was a conference the Govt. of India bagged for the first time since its inception in 1935 to becoming the first event management company of India to develop a Franchising model in the event management space. We are helping create more and more entrepreneurs in the event management space by teaching them and giving them the systems and strategies to build a successful customer value centric, team-centric and purpose-driven business.

Today our dreams have gone beyond crafting our client's dreams, crafting our team's dreams and our own dream to contributing to the world we live in. As DreamCraft we are driven to support children from the slums of Bangalore and help them get access to high quality education so that they can gain the power to dream and realize their dreams. We stand with and support Building Blocks – an NGO which is doing remarkable work in this space. Seeing these children gain access to quality education is the biggest joy of our life.

For me DreamCraft is not just the name of my company but the mission of my life. I get my high out of helping people gain the faith to have a dream and go after it. I believe being a dreamer and working to achieve those dreams is the duty of every human. The biggest difference anyone can make to this planet is to fulfil their dreams and inspire others to fulfil their own. That probably is the best prayer and the best way of honouring the Creator!

Bhakti Sanghavi

Bhakti Sanghavi is an entrepreneur, philanthropist and event manager based in Bangalore, India. She has been in the event management space since 2007 and has to her credit over 600 events designed and delivered for more than 150 organizations. She has co-founded and built DreamCraft Events and Entertainment as a leading brand in the corporate event management space in India and also is the first event management company to have a franchising model to help newer event managers to start-up and scale up rapidly.

Bhakti is also the founder and Chief Creator at Bhakti Sanghavi Signature Weddings – a niche wedding planning company. She is known to design and execute impeccable theme based weddings and has done so for close to a decade.

In addition to her event management business, Bhakti is also a philanthropist supporting Building Blocks India – a NGO committed to providing free high quality education for children from economically backward families who are living in the slums. Her dream is to support the funding of the education of at least 100 children every year. Bhakti believes in a quote she borrows from a friend, that if you want to see worried people, you should go to a mall and if you want to see happy smiles, you should go to the slums.

Bhakti is also a student and practitioner of Pranic Healing – a highly evolved and tested system of energy medicine developed by Grand Master Choa Kok Sui that utilizes prana i.e. life-force to balance, harmonize and transform the body's energy processes.

Bhakti is married to her long term friend and business partner – Rajiv Talreja and together they love traveling the world, supporting entrepreneurs grow their business and enjoying the food & culture of different places.

Company Website – www.dreamcraft.co.in
Email Id – info@dreamcraft.co.in
Facebook - https://www.facebook.com/DreamcraftEvents
Personal Email Id – bhakti@dreamcraft.co.in

8

SUCCESS: A CHIMERA

- BY AVINASH SISODE, FOUNDER OF E&G GROUP OF COMPANIES

Success is painstakingly harvested out of failure.

I was born in a small village having population of less than 1000 people, about 400 kms from Mumbai, India. Though born in a farmer family and brought up in a village, I at the age of 22 knew that my entrepreneurial dreams were about to take flight. I started many businesses out of which many turned out to be major curves of learning for me. I consider failure as merely a learning curve for every entrepreneur.

According to me, Entrepreneur is someone in whose brain some idea to solve some issue of the society or community pops up and he or she starts dreaming about that idea, and one day start business based on this. If I have to encapsulate in a few words, the phenomenal potential of human resources, then I would say, 'together we can create miracles'. This has been my guiding principle ever since I became an entrepreneur. With human beings becoming more and more individualistic and isolated from one another, the fabric of society is tearing apart. Handholding at the micro level and empowering entire communities go a long way in promoting progress and development. All my endeavors, be it incepting and nurturing start-ups or spearheading community projects, have drawn nourishment from this strong belief.

E&G Group of Companies, the first of which was founded in 2008 has today grown to become a conglomerate of 9 companies operating in the areas of construction, real estate, hospitality, education and IT. The hardship and failures that I have gone through prior to tasting success are the cornerstones of this business empire. At the age of 22, however, I knew I wanted to become an entrepreneur. On a lighter note, if I have to talk in numbers, I have failed more number of times than I have succeeded. Nevertheless, it's true. Those were testing times. If I look back I realize how strong I must have been to have not quit and to have persevered until I found success. I have failed about 16 times in business ventures. I must share two of these experiences that were the biggest blows financially and in terms of ideation.

Success: A Chimera

With a diploma in civil engineering, I started my career as a Maharashtra government contractor for building roads and bridges. I was carrying back a hefty paycheck and the going was good. In 1998-99 the urge to do something new took over. The Internet was the buzzword of the day and I shifted focus to the information technology industry. All I knew about computers were the CTRL, ALT and DEL keys on the keyboard!

I started a cyber cafe in my city Jalgaon, where I also offered computer-related courses. Aptech and NIIT approached me to take up their franchise. I wanted to create my own franchise brand. My friends opined that Mumbai or Pune would be a better market for the venture than Jalgaon. I shifted to Pune in 1999, established a training company investing all my savings, and created the requisite course material. The going was good and I was working for 16-18 hours a day with the dream of establishing the franchise model at the pan-India level. We had worked out the entire brand building exercise. We had hired mini-buses, booked hotels, and were traveling from city to city doing road shows and we were about to launch in 15 days.

A front-page news report in Times Of India destroyed our business completely. It read that 50,000 'pink slips' were issued in the US and that marked the beginning of the burst of the IT bubble. I had staked all my earnings. Everything vanished in a day. I was reduced to null. I shut down the company and continued to live in Pune on the money I made by selling the infrastructure. For 6 months I did nothing. The failure had taken over me completely. I had seen failures before too but none compared to this.

I was just surviving. I tried my hand at a couple of other random business ventures, which failed. I did a course in Mumbai, which raised my hope and confidence. I realized that there were so many opportunities waiting for me in my own city. However, I was reluctant to explore fearing the reactions of family, friends, and community the community at large.

I found an opening in the construction business. We were three partners. We had to convert agricultural land to residential plots and sell them. We needed initial funds. I approached my father. But he flatly refused help. All my attempts to convince my father failed. Today, I understand that he couldn't trust me. Finally with the help of my elder brother I convinced my father to pledge his property as collateral for a bank loan. I promised that if I failed to pay up, then I would forsake my rights on the ancestral property.

With a Rs. 5,16,000 bank loan, I started the business. We sold the plots and I paid the first installment to the bank on time. The next year the bank harassed me to pay up the entire loan amount. I did not understand. The loan tenure was a 7-year period and it was now barely a year and a half. I learned later from the bank that my father was forcing the bank to recover the loan as quickly as possible. I paid back the whole amount in the next 2 months and I started with the next construction project.

I used convincing power with those land lords and it was not a good period for construction business also but I created such a network of people who would help me to sell. That was working well and everything was going good, I had earned lot of money and I was in less contact with the family.

One fine day my father came home and all these was going on that there was no one to help me when everything was going bad with me and now people come to me. As he entered inside he hugged me tight and he said that he is very proud of me and cried profusely. After 30 mins. I calmed him down and then I asked what happened. He said, "I went to one of your sites and inquired about the row houses scheme that you have launched. He had enquired about the entire residential township and was very impressed with it and came straight to my home to meet me.

You are a diamond and the only son who is a real gem." I was very happy to hear him praise as every entrepreneur feels very happy when he is appreciated by his father.

He also went on to explain that he didn't want to give him money just like that as he wants me to see succeed in life and be responsible. He also said that it is my blessing to you that you become one of the best people this country has ever seen. I still remember each and every word he uttered. He also said that now I am free from the worry of what will happen to our next 7 generations. He said "all best will happen because you as a responsible son is going to cause all great for next 7 generations".

I belong to a very well to-do family and have lot of ancestral properties too. From that day with those blessings I can see it get materialized.

Turning Point

After all these failures, I think the events of 2004 were Godsent. I felt I had finally connected with my inner self and ever since my profession and my mission for life merged. I realized that I like working with people, in a group and I would love to create something mega i.e. on a big scale. The same year, one day I abruptly sat down with a diary and wrote continuously for four days. I tried to gain a perspective on my life. My past, my present, where I stand, what are my assets--professional and personal qualities, people, etc., and my future roadmap. Today, I realize I had actually drawn up a blueprint of my business. At that time I did not realize this fact. I wanted to start this new business with new business module was focused on entrepreneurial development in Nasik in 2005 or in 2006, but the journey of business carried my dream to 2008. Finally in 2008, I started a company called E&G Global Estates with my wife and brother-in-law. I was the solo player in the beginning; sitting in my 300 sq.ft. office on the second floor of the building. Only few of my friends turned up in a while, but nothing happened to elevate my business hopes for 8 months. I was new to this city and I could not get a yard of land anywhere here. The company focused on creating residential communities in the lap of nature.

Things changed after few months. Kalpatharu Hills, a residential community in the midst of nature, in Nasik, was our first project. This project included farmhouses, nature homes, second homes etc.; as I love nature and Nashik has a wonderful climate. The next was the Green Valley Resort in 2010 and then Green field and Green court Resort. Over the next couple of years, we were a core team of 5 directors and I had established myself in real estate and hospitality industry. This is how the initial journey of E&G began.

In 2010, I established E&G Capital Consultancy Pvt. Ltd., which offered investment-related consultancy in real estate and other business areas and E&G Ventures Pvt. Ltd., which was a group consultancy on all aspects of business, especially strategy and operations.

Roadmap for entrepreneurial success

I was once again on the look- out for something new to do and all along I had felt that support and mentorship could go a long way in nurturing budding entrepreneurs. I participated in a course in Panchgani, Mahabaleshwar near Pune and realized that my real passion was to create, nurture and support budding entrepreneurs. Just like my partners and I, most entrepreneurs resort to the trial and error method and thus go through a lot of hardship making many mistakes on the way. My co-founders had also experienced failures and success, so we wanted to help the budding entrepreneurs through our experiences. There is really no roadmap to entrepreneurial success that one can follow. I felt; why not create a crystal clear pathway for success in business and life. The idea was to create, support and nurture entrepreneurs. It took me a year to convert this idea into a precise formula.

In 2011, I created a course called E3 - Entrepreneurs Energy Excellence, and offered it free of cost initially. The course was a huge success. The first batch trained 21 participants. The program was designed to educate participants in entrepreneurship modules across Tier 2 and Tier 3 cities in India. Most participants were primarily from Tier 3 cities and include farmers, doctors, small business owners and so on. WE empowered them with various aspects of entrepreneurship like personality development, teaching how to connect their passion to a sustainable business module and even help them to build and present their business plans to potential investors. WE have successfully empowered more than 100,000 people by changing their mindset about Entrepreneurship and managed to create a social change in Tier 2 and Tier 3 cities and the society.

Inspired, I started the E&G Innovative Education in 2012, a company focused on offering education to entrepreneurs. My purpose was to give not only linear education but breakthrough education; which will influence people's lives in all aspects. The company has, to date, groomed and launched approximately 1,200 individual entrepreneurs. We offer a special module for women entrepreneurs, the W3, as well. A few of these entrepreneurs have engaged me as their mentor. Under my mentorship, they have experienced sustained growth; some have doubled their profits; others have replicated their business in other locations.

I started a couple of more businesses thereafter. I realized that I didn't want to own and run every business that I started. My core strength lies in conceiving new business ideas and translating them into viable business establishments. Leadership is my forte. Therefore, after I start an enterprise, I find the right people to take it forward, support them in every possible way until they can fly solo, and then I smoothly hand it over entirely to them and I exit. All this happened through self-realization and the realization of my strengths and weaknesses.

Therefore, the business model allows us to share the stakes with the youngsters. We offer the stakes, free of cost and allow them to grow and prosper. Our mantra is those who have money will invest money and those who have skills will leverage their skills and grow. We handhold new entrepreneurs mentor them and support their growth. This is not social entrepreneurship. You may call it social plus business entrepreneurship.

Last year I established a company called Entrepreneurs Network and Education Business Club. The business model is similar to that of Airbnb, the biggest rental platform that doesn't own a single property; or Apple, the highest profit maker without owning a single store. So the Club aims to be the biggest Club for entrepreneurs the world over, without actually owning and operating a club. We will be a network of business clubs dedicated to networking and growth of entrepreneurs. Again, the purpose behind all this is the theme- 'Let us grow together'. We are launching it in the 3rd quarter of 2016.

Another business I am working on is related to handkerchiefs. In the western world, while there are numerous exclusive brands dedicated to formal shirts, tee shirts, trousers, business suits and even accessories such as ties, cufflinks etc, there is not a single brand specializing in premium handkerchiefs. So I have launched the brand, Kerfs and it has been received very well. We are operating it as a women entrepreneurship model for homemakers, who can create a movement by roping in other women members of the family and extended family. We are getting business enquiries from the UAE and the US. We are launching a brand in Tea- an Ayurvedic tea- which is a unique product.

Mantra for Success

Having strong belief in 'I can be rich' is the real key and each one of us has that right, ability and desire
According to me being Rich is having the assets for taking care of you, your family and your generations and freedom to create liabilities

Holistic Organic growth

'Let us grow together.' I believe that true organic development can occur in an entrepreneur's life only by growing with others. My story of entrepreneurship as you seen begins with this simple truth.

Networking

At the beginning, I spoke about the immense potential of human resources coming together and working for a common purpose. The single most important prerequisite for success is networking. Bringing together people from different professional backgrounds with varied skill-sets ushers in novel ideas. Each will contribute their specialization. Some may invest. Others may ideate. Someone else may execute. If we help others, they will also help us. If you want something from the world, start giving it. Connecting with people, and connecting people from varied walks of life is something that inspires me. **Consistent focused actions, taken with ease and grace creates miracle** and I believe that together we can create miracles.

Perseverance

Failure is a part of life. If you want to be an entrepreneur you have to continue forever, with the strong belief that you will succeed one day. Most entrepreneurs fail not because of failure of a business idea or poor execution but simple because they are not willing to try and try harder. Besides, every failure is only a learning experience. This experience, no business school can ever teach you.

Mentorship

It is always better to find a mentor who can help you in your entrepreneurial journey. I am eternally grateful to my mentor Mr. T. R. Doongaji, from the prestigious TATA Group of companies. I cherish my interactions with Robert Kiyosaki, Jerry Roberts, Werner Erhards, Michel Jenson, Ratan Tata, Les Brown among others. I have learned a lot on how we as a nation can promote the entrepreneurial spirit among the youth.

I urge youngsters to become innovative entrepreneurs. There is immense potential in our country for youngsters. The economy is vibrant and on the upward trend. When I made my foray into business the climate for young first generation entrepreneurs was almost inclement. Business was reserved only for those hailing from business families or those with a big bank balance. However, today the start-up ecosystem is very conducive. There are people/organizations ready to fund out of the box ideas. Economic policies are favorable. Globalization gives you the world on a silver platter. The world is yours to take!

Leveraging Life's Full Potential

Currently, I am playing a key role in framing the policy on entrepreneurship for Govt. of Maharashtra, India.

I am also authoring a book titled, 'The Next 7 Generations will never forgive you." I am an avid reader on various topics. I love to travel, meet, and interact with successful people. I like to engage myself with the society around me. I hate to isolate myself as a businessman who cannot think beyond his turf. Besides, I derive great joy in sharing my learning and experiences. I regularly write in the newspapers to keep in touch with society. I have written articles on Entrepreneurship in newspapers and magazines

I have been incredibly influenced by many great people, some my contemporaries, others, great saints of yore.

- The monk, Gautama Buddha gave everything to the world 2500 years back. His technique of Vipasana meditation, which I have learned has had a great impact on my evolution as a human being and influenced the whole world greatly. He is my first mentor It is a technique of self-improvement through self-observation.

- King Shivaji- He reigned in Maharashtra in the era of Aurangzeb. He created an eco system that benefitted all. I am greatly influenced by the way he created and expanded his empire and the way he treated his dedicated followers and fellow-leaders.
- OSHO's teaching have inspired me to push my limits and I have been able to discover and use my potential to the fullest--to live life to the fullest.
- Robert Kiyosaki's books, especially. Rich dad's series first 3 books have taught me a lot about the nuances of business. They have honed my attitude and behavior as a businessman. I got my definitions of assets and liabilities from him.
- Swami Ramdev- He is creating a new domain in entrepreneurship. I call it ' GuruPreneurship.' I have learnt from him that it is all about 'you'; i.e. your health- bodily and mental. If you are healthy and happy you can make others happy.

I have got inspiration from many other people; people from my native place, my family and my colleagues. I have learnt a lot of things from them. I think that if you are human you can learn anything. So, be a human being first.

Several awards have come my way. They only help me focus better and ignite me to find ways to empowering communities. The Rotary Club award bestowed on me during the Vidharba Rotary Club Conference is perhaps the most satisfying. I had spearheaded a social project aimed at the childless and the award was made in recognition of this project. The E&G Charitable Foundation, founded in 2011 is committed to the upliftment of the underprivileged in society through education.

Currently, the E & G Group has the following companies under its administrative guidance, among others:

- E&G Global Estates Ltd.
- E&G Capital Consultancy Pvt., Ltd.
- E&G Ventures Pvt. Ltd.
- E&G Resorts Pvt. Ltd.
- E & G Charitable Foundation
- E & G Innovative Education Pvt. Ltd.
- ENE International Business Clubs Pvt. Ltd.
- Wealth Zone Realtors LLP.
- Wealth Zone Concept Clothing LLP
- Wealth House Real Estate LLP

I have fostered the following values in all my group companies:
- Credibility
- Trust
- Excellence
- Innovation
- Environmental protection

I have a clear vision for the future of E&G Group of Companies. I want the company to grow into a conglomerate of 25 companies and having 100 plus directors. employing thousands of people. Keeping this in mind, for the next fiscal, we have opened up two IPOs for two of our companies. This is perhaps the first Business house in india to offer two IPOs in the same fiscal year. I am very clear that our growth and expansion strategies are entirely transparent and ethical. E&G Groups all directors and team members are consistently working to make it happen.

I am a true believer of peace and I want world peace. I believe that, this country of mine will give peace to the world. We never invaded any region on this earth but fought with the invaders every time. This is our history. People of India are loving people. this is the country of true love. If we rule the world i.e. if we become the financial superpower peace will be automatically restored on this earth. This is my philosophy.

If we want India to be financial superpower of the world we will have to encourage entrepreneurship. It is only these entrepreneurs who can contribute to the GDP of this country. Till 200-250 years back we were the leading economy of the world and India's contribution to the world economy was huge that means we have experienced the golden era in the very recent past. So we are used to it and we know how to get there. It is in our genes and if each one of us can create one male and one female entrepreneur in our entire lifetime then that will be our great contribution in building this nation and to make India again living the golden era . For that, **My mission is to make Indian Entrepreneurs capital of the world.**

Avinash Sisode

🏠 G-3, New Shivsagar Society, Near HDFC Bank, Thatte Nagar, Gangapur – College Link Road, Nashik, Maharashtra - 422 005

☎ 0253 – 2311879   📱 +91 9860643999 www.eandg.in

Group Chairman & Managing Director, E & G Group of companies

Group Values:

- Credibility
- Trust
- Excellence
- Innovation

- Environment

The group has following companies under its administrative guidance:

1. Presently Stake Holder, E&G Global Estates Ltd. since inception i.e. 21/05/2008

Company's Vision: "To generate wealth for all by creating communities in nature"

Activity: Civil Construction, Construction of luxury villas blending with Nature

2. Presently Director, E&G Capital Consultancy Pvt., Ltd., Stake Holder since inception i.e. 05/03/2010

Company's Vision: "Being consistent wealth creator for investors through transparent investments in real estate and other businesses"

Activity: Consultancy in Investments in business and real Estate.

3. Managing Director, E&G Ventures Pvt. Ltd. since inception i.e. 13/10/2010

Company's Vision: "Make investments that impact human existence positively".
Activity: In groups' advisory role on all aspects of business esp. on strategy and improvements in operations.

4. Managing Director, E&G Resorts Pvt. Ltd. Stake Holder since inception i.e.13/06/2011.

Company's Vision: "To provide unique experience of luxury & fulfillment with nature"

Activity: Operations and maintenance of Resorts and Villas.

5. Promoter, E & G Charitable Foundation, Founded in 05/09/2011

Company's Vision: "To Draw inspiration from Nature. Give it back to mankind"

Activity: Education and uplifting under-privileged

6. Managing Director, E & G Innovative Education Pvt. Ltd. since inception, i.e. 03/10/2012

Company's Vision: "Educate people to live fulfilled life"

Activity: Innovative Education on Business personality development such as E3 for men and W3 for women

7. Chairman, ENE International Business Clubs Pvt. Ltd. since inception i.e. 20/03/2015

Company's Vision: "To Create, Support and Nurture Entrepreneurs"

Activity: Business education, Entrepreneurs' business networking and mentoring.

Publications:

- Every Wednesday articles on" Development" in Maharashtra Times.

- In 2014, "Vasant Vyakhyan" articles on Entrepreneurship and "Marathi Man" in different newspapers like Gavakari, Maharashtra Times, Deshdoot, Sakal, Divya Marathi, Nashik Punyanagari, Lokmat etc.

- A big article on Kumbhmela-Opportunities and Challenges in Maharashtra Times newspaper.

- "Next 7 Generations will never forgive you….." A book being written by Mr. Avinash Sisode. It's in progress to be published.

Awards:

- Saturday Club Entrepreneur of the year(2013)
- Divya Marathi Award for Green Project (2012)
- Award from Deep Stambha Foundation for empowerment (2012)
- Rotary Best Social Project Award(2004)
- Felicitated as one of the best community Project in Rotary, Nagpur Conference

9

WHAT KITE ARE YOU FLYING?

- BY VIVEK AGARWAL, FOUNDER OF GPA GROUP

On a windy day in the month of March, the Mayor of a town decided to take a stroll across the park. While on his stroll he came across a small boy who was flying what the Mayor thought was the biggest and most striking of kites he had ever seen.

It soared so high up in the sky that the Mayor was sure that it could be seen from far even in the cities next to theirs. The Mayor had not seen anything so remarkable ever. He knew that his city did not have anything as spectacular as this kite so he decided to award a "key to the city" to the one who was responsible for such a beautiful thing.

And he asked, "Who is responsible for flying this kite?"

"I am," came the answer from the little boy who held on to the kite with all his might. The boy said, "I made this huge kite myself, with my own hands. I painted all of the colorful pictures on it, and I fly it!"

The Mayor was impressed by the boy's efforts when suddenly the wind chimed.

"I am responsible for the beautiful kite flying in the sky," it said. "It is my breeze that keeps this big kite flying in the sky, looking so beautiful. Unless I blow on it, it will not fly at all. I fly it!"

Another contender for the award was the Kite's tail. "Not so," it said. "I make it sail and give it stability against the wind's blowing gusts. Without me, the kite would spin out of control and nobody, not even the boy could save it from crashing to the earth. I fly the kite!"

Like the many contenders who claim to be responsible for the beauty of the kite that flies in the sky, there are many stakeholders in any success story.

TEAM

Success is never about a single person. While we congratulate and celebrate the leaders we tend to forget those invisible heroes who stand by his/her side making him the leader that he/she is. No leader is successful without his team. A "team" is not just people who work at the same time in the same place but it is a group of very different individuals who share a commitment to working together to achieve common goals. Most likely they are not all equal in experience, talent or education, but they are equal in one vitally important way, their commitment to the good of the organization. I am a staunch believer in the spirit of 'oneness'. If people are working together as members of a solid team, whether it is a family, a group of friends, in a partnership, as employees and employers, it eventually leads to success in life.

In reality, everyone is part of the team that flies the beautiful big kite! Teamwork is what matters the most for real success. It is important to me that while I continue to grow in terms of business those who are with me should also benefit from it.

If you ask me about my leadership approach—I will say; TEAM – Team Enables Achieve Miracles. I sincerely believe in the strength of togetherness, of oneness. If you asked me who made me an entrepreneur, I'd would say my passion and commitment but if you ask me who made me a successful entrepreneur, its my team..

A startup can become successful only if it has employees who are loyal and hardworking. Loyalty and rock-solid work ethics can help you do anything. Combine this with passion and you have the incredible power to change the world.

I believe that without my team I could not have achieved anything. I share a very strong bond with my employees and this has given me a lot of courage and strength to surge ahead. I think that every organization has to adapt itself to the new demands and change itself constantly by investing in new learning for its employees.

Take an example of a child who just started to take tiny little steps. His success is climbing that very first step on the staircase. The baby doesn't see the entire staircase. For him, success is that first step. Most importantly, success need not necessarily have anything to do with money. A tiny step toward a larger goal is success. My definition of success is to have 50,000 employees by 2030. I'd like to do it sooner, but I believe that 2030 is more realistic. If you have a strong team by your side, any dream is achievable.

The Birth of a Big Dream

I want to build GPA as a diverse, sustainable and profitable business model. I want to create employment for the youth and contribute towards the betterment of the society. The core values that drive me in my day-to-day business are simple and they are Integrity, Precision, Compassion and Promise. These 4 values mean a lot to me. GPA stands for the name of my father, Shri Govind Prasad Agrawal. Obviously, I chose the name as a tribute to him. Another person, I look up to is my uncle, Mr. Bijay Agarwal who is an inspiration to me. It is to these two individuals that I turn to in times of crisis for advice and guidance even to this day. There have been other people also who have contributed towards my success and I would like to acknowledge them too.

This dream starts from my childhood. I have grown up seeing my father build everything from scratch. Entrepreneurship was in my blood. I believe that instead of waiting for the right opportunities, one needs to create them. I started gaining experience by selling tea and bhujiya in college. I also did internship in Himalaya publications as a proofreader. I used to sit there till 12 at midnight after my college and realized how hard is to earn money. When I used to go home in holidays I used to sit in the office and observe my father and sharpened my business sense. These experiences have been my school of training. But everything has not been as rosy as it sounds. After completing my masters at Nottingham University Business School, I decided to come back to India to start my own venture. I decided to take the plunge on 27th of November 2008. When I told my father about my decision to move out into a big city and start my own business, he was hesitant but soon agreed to support me. I convinced him, reasoning that I would try it for "2 years and if nothing happened I would return". In my heart, I gave myself no choice but successes .

I moved to Calcutta and rented an apartment there and had only the basic necessities and a laptop. Every day I used to travel by metro and even walk to short distances to save auto fare. It was not at all easy for me in Kolkata though my father could afford all luxury very easily; I wanted to earn them myself. I used to go from one office to another and wait for hours to pitch my idea. I was not taken very seriously and was told that I was too young to start anything of my own. It went on like that for about 7-8 months. Luckily when I imported the first consignment of sugar from Brazil with the help of one of my brother, I made a good profit. I was able to return the money that I had borrowed from my father with interest and the rest I invested in stock market.

Three Decisions

Three major decisions have been instrumental in shaping my life. First and foremost was the decision to go abroad to study. I was the first in my family to venture out. That gave me an opportunity to interact with different kind of people. The second decision was to go through the struggling phase when I could have easily taken help from my father. During that time, I could not afford a laptop, a car or any such luxury. I did not give up or loose heart. This was a good learning experience for me. Thirdly, running and sustaining the first venture is something that had a profound impact on me. The decision to sustain my first venture against all odds gave me the courage to go ahead and think big in life.

However, some decisions are very painful to take. The hardest decision was to go my own way. I had the option of running my father's business. Leaving my family and going elsewhere was hard. It was such a difficult decision that I labored over it for twenty days and argued with my father. This incident made me realize how much my father loved me. In contrast, though I've had to make many tough business decisions, I've always been able to find the solution that works best for me. I am passionate about what I do so I always have a reason to enjoy my work. For instance, I enjoy travelling a lot and never loose an opportunity to strike a conversation or learn something new.

The Best Part of Being an Entrepreneur

The best part of being an entrepreneur is breaking new ground and being the first at inventing new technology or creating a new market opportunity where none existed before. It also gives chance to stand up for what you believe in, and spread the word and it is the truest expression of myself. I can take the long view and set myself on a path of learning and growth that allows me to accomplish the change I want to see in the world. It allows me to express my personal core values through my business activities. It certainly involves hard work, commitment and responsibility. But if you love what you do, you will always be highly motivated.

I consider myself to be a social entrepreneur and I do find time to spend with those who need social support and encouragement. Through the initiatives of SUIT (Societal Upliftment Initiative Trust), I get to spend some quality time with children and it gives me an opportunity to inspire and motivate them. I like to share my thoughts and ideas through articles, speeches etc. in an effort to reach out to maximum number of people.

To any young and aspiring entrepreneur, I would like to advice the following

1. Believe in yourself- because if you don't no one else will.
2. Build a strong team – Team Enables to Achieve Miracles
3. Be honest to everyone including your self.

Skydiving and Business

Skydiving has taught me many things and each time I do it, I've realized how important life is. It also gives me an opportunity to introspect and correct any wrong doings. As a result, I believe being adventurous is good for entrepreneurs. Running a business is like skydiving: it can be hard and scary. They say a skydiver doesn't get a second chance, and I've seen businessmen who end up losing while trying to grow their businesses.

People don't see you as successful until you've already made it to the top. They don't see your struggles or how much effort is involved in your success. However, struggles and failures go hand-in-hand. When you're a failure, you struggle to succeed again!

Perseverance is a key element to succeed. Imagine the tip of an iceberg--that's success. The bulk of the berg is beneath the ice, and people can't see all the endless struggles you've been through to get where you are. They only see the tip of that success i.e. the iceberg without really seeing the underlying dedication, sacrifices, efforts, and failures. I have had my share of struggles and that motivated me to put SUIT together. It's a non-profit organization operating in five states. We identify families whose monthly income is less than Rs 5,000 and support education of their children. We also provide them books and clothes to ensure they learn something. I know I can't educate all the children in India, but I believe its my responsibility to give back to the society.

The Award

Recently I was awarded the Young Entrepreneur of the Year 2015 (India) organised by US-based "Entrepreneur Magazine" and also received Rajiv Gandhi Excellence Award of Emerging Brand of the Year – MTECH Mobiles. That's the biggest recognition I've ever received for what I do. It has boosted my confidence so much that I want to do more things and compound my success.

One Little Thing

There's one more thing I want to share: Do not succumb to disappointment from struggles and failures. This will happen, period.

What I always say to those who are willing to listen is that if you've failed once, do not believe that is the end! There will always be a second chance, and even a third one, and plenty more after that. In this competitive world, we must be fighters and have the ability to bounce back from any situation. I'm sure that you are one of those who choose to WIN.

Vivek Agarwal

An alumina of Nottingham university business School, Mr. Vivek Agarwal is a young achiever in the Indian Business Industry. He bagged the Young Entrepreneur Award in the year 2015 and also received Rajiv Gandhi Excellence Award of Emerging Brand of the Year – MTECH Mobiles. Vivek Agarwal is the Chairman and Managing Director of GPA Group, and aims build the group as a diverse, sustainable and profitable business model. The core values that drive him in his day-to-day business are Integrity, Precision, Compassion and Promise. GPA stands for the name of his father, Shri Govind Prasad Agrawal. Obviously, he chose the name as a tribute to him. Another person, he looks up to is his uncle, Mr. Bijay Agrawal. It is to these two individuals that he turns to in times of crisis for advice and guidance even to this day.

He founded Leverage Group in the year 2010 a real estate company, which is in the business of constructing residential and commercial properties as well as consultancy in real estate. After successful completion of 5 projects in Nagpur, Leverage Group in now building townships of approx. 300 flats and has 5 more projects in pipeline. With considerable experience in the real estate industry under his belt, he has ambitious plans for growth and expansion, and he is actively involved in setting and executing company's strategic goals.

He is also the Managing Director of M Tech Informatics Ltd which embarks on an ambitious journey to provide Quality affordable innovation along with a promise to deliver high end after sales service to the Indian market. Under his leadership, the company bagged the Rajiv Gandhi Excellence Award for Emerging Brand in the year 2015. In span of 4 years, M-Tech has turnover of INR 100 crore. In an expansion mode, M Tech has started its own manufacturing unit in Baddi, HP.

The Belgachi Tea Estate, which was acquired by him in the year 2010 when it was declared a sick unit, is now producing 1.5 million kg of tea every year and also provides employment to 1500 people. It is now a profit-making venture.

Vivek believes in promoting young talent and he has invested as a venture capitalist, he invested in brandbazooka.com, which is a marketing and advertising company. It has worked with more than 100 brands from various verticals. He is also an investor and a mentor in Skycandle.in that caters to home decor segment. He has been instrumental in the turnaround of both these ventures.

In 2015 he stepped into the world of e-commerce and launched comparemunafa.com. It is the only online portal that offers price comparison, product discovery, coupons and deals and Munafa points (similar to cashback) with value added features such as price drop alert and price graph on a single platform.

As a believer in the spirit of oneness, he shares the benefits of growth in his business with the underprivileged through his initiative called SUIT. He is one of the co-founders of SUIT which works towards educating the underprivileged children. Spread across 5 states (10 districts) and with the support of 10 implementing partners, SUIT has been able to support the education of more than 500 children. It has initiated 7 informal education centers, 1 evening class and 11-night class centers. SUIT has transformed more than 25 villages through health education for disease prevention through various activities, which include competitions in drawing, general knowledge, health awareness campaigns etc.

10

PURSUIT OF SUCCESS

- BY DR. SUNIL KUMAR, MD, DNB(RD), FRCR(UK), CONSULTANT RADIOLOGIST AND FOUNDER OF ADD-ON SCANS AND LABS

Pursuit of success is like running a marathon.

"You are your greatest asset. Put your time, effort and money into training, grooming, and encouraging your greatest asset." These words from millionaire businessman, Tom Hopkins have been my guiding principle in my journey through life.

Hailing from a small village, from a middle class family, I have had to chart the course of my life right from the beginning. With no proper guidance and little financial aid, I have had to make my decisions and earn a living all along. The initial years of life I spent in Chickmagalur and Halebeedu in Karnataka. As with most kids who gain the primary education in their mother tongue and then abruptly shift to English medium schools for primary or middle school education, I had all the apprehensions and anxieties that come with being suddenly thrown into a new ambience. My aunt who was my caregiver during kindergarten remembers that I was very bold and confident till such time as when I moved into an English school, after which, I grew increasingly shy and introverted and lost all confidence. Without an idiom to express myself, a sense of inferiority perhaps crept in and was to remain for a long time gnawing at my self-esteem. This is also the story of thousands of kids in India who shift from a school where the medium of instruction is in the regional language to an English-medium school. Such kids mostly come from families, in which parents are uneducated, or at best are have some basic education in a local language.

In high school, things started taking a turn for the better. I was nominated the class leader and suddenly the confidence that I had lost, began to return. I realized that when given a responsibility or when under pressure, I could push myself to perform. That is when I felt that if I wanted to, I could change myself. Yet, till I completed my 10th grade, I couldn't figure out how I could change myself.

Perhaps, the desire to live independently was the first step towards the change I wanted to see in myself. My parents were simple, innocent folk. They were not worldly-wise to guide me in life or education. I am very thankful to them for funding my basic education despite financial constraint and supporting me in all the decisions I was to take thereafter. The immense trust they reposed in me, certainly played a big role albeit subconsciously, in my journey towards change.

I moved to Davangere to pursue two years of pre-university

(PU) education. Now again, I found myself among students who were state-level rank holders and who had a very clear vision for their future. I was still an average student, who hated Math. I loved Biology and that's when I nursed the dream of studying to become a doctor. I was naive enough to believe that love for a subject was enough to pursue a career. However, this naiveté eventually fuelled the passion and dedication, which alone ushers in success.

I passed the PU exam in first class. I was averse to a course in Engineering because of my dislike for Math. I did not get through the entrance exam for MBBS. Left with little choice, I decided to return to my village to lead the life of a farmer. Nevertheless, I landed a seat for BDS. I pursued the course for a few months before I decided that it was not my cup of tea simply because I didn't like the course. On the other hand, I realized that I had the potential to complete the course. In addition, if I could complete BDS, then I could certainly complete MBBS. So these couple of months had instilled new confidence in me, also because I was chosen Mr. Fresher at the fresher's party and later as the monitor of my class.

I moved to Mangalore and decided to appear once again for the MBBS entrance exam. I found myself among peers who possessed the wherewithal to 'buy' a seat if required. I had only myself to depend on; I was my only asset. The next six years, I burned the midnight oil. The library was where I spent the nights. I had, in fact, kept a pillow there, to catch a few winks in the wee hours of the morning, before I could head to lectures. At the end of those six years, I was at the forefront of my peers. I grew to be so confident in theory and practical, that during a practical exam I picked up a distinct murmur in the heart of a patient I was examining, which even the invigilating professor had missed. With great confidence, I reported the same to him. He could also trace it. After the exam he called me to congratulate me, but also warned me to beware of over-confidence.

While most students studied prescribed texts end to end, and went no further, I would never be satisfied by mere theory. Reading a textbook is like gathering a lot of data. Now, how do you convert this accumulated data into knowledge? Data translates into knowledge only when it can be applied in practice in a context. So I would try very hard to apply what I had learnt during practical sessions. I discovered I was good in applied medicine.

Another critical skill that shaped my intellect was the art of questioning and probing. In this, my mentor was a senior by two years, Dr. Shiva Reddy. There used to be a great camaraderie between juniors and seniors. They often played the role of 'friend, philosopher and guide '. He had a peculiar way of teaching juniors. He would throw a lot of questions at us and encouraged us to think and provoke us by challenging common sense notions and assumptions. He ignited in us critical thinking; he taught us to push ourselves to the brink to find answers. He opened our minds to the world. In the words of Robert Kiyosaki, businessman, and motivational speaker, 'The most successful people are the one who ask questions. They're always learning. They're always growing. They're always pushing.'

I opted Radiology for the three-year MD course. I missed my family the most during this period since I rarely visit them. I survived on a meager Rs. 2,500 a month. Despite the struggle, this period was when I discovered my passion for Radiology. I allowed myself to be completely consumed by the subject. I read every book I could lay my hand on related to Radiology. I barely focused on the prescribed syllabus. I didn't attend too many classes either. I was busy quizzing! Participating and winning every quiz competition on Radiology. Peers came to me for help rather than attending classes or asking professors. I passed the MD course as a University rank holder.

During 2009-10, I joined work in Trivandrum. I earned a handsome salary of Rs. 2 lakh a month. I repaid all the loans my father had taken for my studies. Then, I didn't know what to do with so much money. Despite the good salary, the desire to learn in a larger setup and gain greater exposure goaded me to shift base to Bangalore. I joined Fortis hospital and worked from 8 am to 8 pm shifting between their facilities on Bannerghatta Road and Cunningham Road, for half the salary! Here, in addition to gaining exposure and fine-tuning my skills, I also understood how processes were built and executed.

In the meantime, I appeared for DNB examination in Trivandrum medical college and cleared the exam in first attempt. The examiners were very much impressed with my case presentation and with way I could tackle the questions. I also applied for FRCR(Fellow Royal College of Radiology, London) and failed in my first attempt out of sheer overconfidence. I hadn't studied their examination methodology. While in India, education is focused on acquiring knowledge, in the U.K, the focus is on applying the knowledge acquired. Although I was good at applied medicine, I realized I had to get better. In the absence of a mentor, my practice became my mentor. I applied everything I had learnt when I diagnosed and treated patients at the hospital and learnt everything on my own. Now, I was able to clear the FRCR. Discipline, work ethic, and professionalism are some of the qualities I picked up during my stint in England.

After finishing FRCR, I had the choice of a career in England. The idea of wanting to do something on my own had germinated in my mind. For lack of a clear idea, I joined a US-based teleradiology services company under Dr. Arjun Kalyan, a true legend in radio diagnosis. The company delivered 98.5% accuracy in radio diagnosis. This is where I understood what quality services actually meant. I was working in shifts that changed every week. I worked mostly night shifts and it was very strenuous. On one such return drive from work, I met with an accident. I had dozed off while driving and my car fell off the flyover. The car was completely mangled. I crawled out of the window. I was in one piece! Nothing short of a miracle. I realized God had given me a second chance. I was living in a grace period. The impulse to establish some venture on my own grew stronger after this incident.

From employee to entrepreneur

I brainstormed with various options with like-minded doctors and finally decided on starting a medical center that would offer the entire spectrum of services from illness to wellness. I started the first medical center called Westgate Medical Centre and Diagnostics. It's been a year and a half and the center has a team of 25 eminent doctors, experts in their respective fields of healthcare. Westgate Medical Centre and Diagnostics provides holistic healthcare that includes prevention, treatment, rehabilitation and health education for patients and their families by touching their lives through quality healthcare delivery. Each department spends a significant amount of time in educating and informing patients regarding disease prevention. We also educate them on how they can proactively improve treatment outcomes.

I was entirely new to entrepreneurship. I learnt all about how a partnership works, how proprietorship works; I also had to pick up the skills required for managing finances, marketing, administration and so on. There were too many things I was trying to master at once, so I started maintaining a journal. I became a keen observer. The minutest details of things that interested me went into my diary. In addition, I tried to implement these things in my business.

After a year and half of starting Westgate medical center, I had reasonable confidence to start another stand alone diagnostics center in Sarjapur road, Bengaluru. It is called add-on Scans and

Labs. It has state of the art medical equipment with world class ambience.

Maintaining the sanctity of my profession while running it as a business enterprise is quite a challenge. The two seem diametrically opposed. Nevertheless, both aspects are integral to the success of my enterprise. While it is not possible to make the world understand that the balance can be maintained without compromising on one or the other or on ethics, I try to make my staff understand this. The cornerstones of my business are the 5 C's:

- **Compassion** - Without compassion you cease to be a doctor. Then you are only a moneymaking machine.
- **Commitment** - Being a service oriented enterprise, especially in the healthcare sector, we are bound by a commitment to our patient's wellbeing.
- **Communication** - We must master the art of articulating, especially when breaking news, both good and bad, to patients or their relatives.
- **Collaboration** - We are a group of people, with diverse skills trying to work together. Without collaboration, the enterprise will fall apart.
- **Consistency** - Consistent service is what ultimately helps retain customers, for they know what to expect and are assured that they will be satisfied.

My wife is the proprietor of the organization. She manages accounts and human resources. She trains our employees once a week, and the employees are expected to make presentations every week, based on which they are given incentives. We also set revenue targets and make our employees understand that targets are important to make the business viable. The fact that the Centre in Basavangudi has been running very well in terms of revenue and in terms of gaining confidence and satisfaction of patients is proof enough. I was motivated to start another medical and diagnostic center on Sarjapur road. I have realized that systematizing process makes replication easy.

My father-in-law has been a great source of strength in my entrepreneurial journey. He is endowed with enormous business acumen and has guided me all along. He hand-held me until I learnt the ropes of business management.

Between 20 and 60

Now I am in my mid-30s. I intend to set up 3 more clinics in the next 3 years. So that will be 5 clinics in 5 years. I am trying to emulate Jack Ma's (Chinese self-made billionaire, Founder, and CEO of Alibaba) advice to young entrepreneurs. He talks about how one can chart out one's life between 20 and 60 years. He advises one to be a good student till 20 to gain knowledge. Before one turns 30, he says one should work in a small organization; because in a big organization you are but a cog in the wheel. In a small enterprise, you tend to have a bird's eye view of the organization. You are in touch with the passion, the dreams of your boss. You get to see the human face of the enterprise. You learn directly from the boss. So which boss you emulate is the crucial factor. Between 30 and 40 you must decide whether you want to become an entrepreneur and if you do, then you must start your business. You must learn and do all that is necessary to establish your business. Between 40 and 50 you must sharpen your existing skills. Between 50 and 60 you must build a team of youngsters or work for them; invest in them, train them, rely on them. Finally, when you are over 60, spend time on yourself! Relax and enjoy.

I strongly believe that all of us have the potential to succeed and achieve. I do not write-off anybody. There will come a time and place when each will discover his true potential. That brings to mind a beautiful quote by Sir Richard Branson, 'People are no different from flowers. If you water them, they flourish. If you are not nice to them, they shrivel up.' I want to pave the way for my employees to grow. I do not wish them to end up as cogs in a wheel. I don't want my employees to be dispensable. I can motivate my employees, I want them to grow along with me and scale up. I want them to bloom rather than wither.

Life is for the long haul

Of late, I have trained hard and started participating in marathons. I have completed about 10 marathons. During one of my early runs, I realized that running was almost like meditation. It is a great stress reliever. The marathon itself stands as a metaphor for one's journey through life. Like life, the marathon run is for the long haul. It doesn't end quickly. Besides, when you run you only look at those ahead of you. They are motivation enough for you to achieve what they have. The time you take to complete the run is of no consequence. The fact that you complete the run makes you a winner. In life too, all of us have the potential to become winners, albeit at different times. Life gives each of us the same chance and opportunity; to become winners at our own pace. The pursuit of success never ends, because the idea of success itself constantly morphs in our mind creating new milestones.

Dr. Sunil Kumar G S

MD, DNB(RD), FRCR(UK), Consultant Radiologist

http://addonhealthcare.com
https://in.linkedin.com/pub/dr-sunil-kumar/67/55b/4bb

Dr. Sunil Kumar is the founder of Add-on Scans and Labs in Bengaluru. He is also the co-founder of Westgate Medical Center and Diagnostics, Bengaluru.

Dr. Sunil is the guest faculty at various medical conferences and CME's due to the fact that he was the University rank holder in MD (RD). He is passionate about quiz competitions and has won a number of contests, apart from running more than 10 marathon events so far.

Dr. Sunil has also been the President of Ashraya Charitable Trust (Blood Bank), goes as a panelist on a regional TV show and has co-authored medical articles.

He is passionate about the healthcare industry and has great ambitions to set up one of the largest healthcare systems in India, which will be known for ethical medical practice and delivering compassionate health care, at an affordable cost.

11

CHANGE FOR HAPPINESS

- BY ASHOK SOOTA, FOUNDER OF HAPPIEST MINDS TECHNOLOGIES PVT. LTD.

Friendship with Change.

Most people take great pride in philosophizing that change is the only constant; they also hate the change when the moment to change arrives. In my life, I embraced change as a friend right from my childhood. My family moved to India from the North-West Frontier in Pakistan during partition and my father who was serving in the army was transferred frequently, and consequently I changed 12 schools by the time I was 12 years old!

When I look back, I think that that was a tremendous

experience for two reasons. First, I got the chance to see the whole country; second, I learnt how to be flexible and agile. I couldn't join a school and say, 'I have exams two months from now and I am expected to study Hamlet, whereas I have studied As You Like It.' I learned how to just get down to things, prepare and do what I had to do.

After completing schooling in the city of Lucknow I went on to do my Bachelor of Engineering degree in Electrical Engineering from the Roorkee University (now IIT, Roorkee). I underwent multiple rounds of interviews to get my first job in Calcutta with Burmah Shell, at that time one of the most sought after employers.

It was a technical job with a well-paid salary and a car, which was a rare luxury for a person in the first year of his career back then. I was less than a few months in the job when my boss' boss retired and suddenly my boss also quit to start his own business and I was overnight given the responsibility to run the entire enterprise. I was offering technical advice to factories in terms of what type of combustion fuels and lubricants to use and what blends would suit their processes. After a while I realized that the product needed no selling. My Divisional Manager once said, with reference to me, that 'we have an enthusiastic young man who has done 11 surveys for new requirements when we are rationing suppliers to existing customers.' So I said to myself, 'What am I doing here?' and within a year I left.

I got a wonderful job with DCM as a Senior Management Trainee, took a significant salary cut, let go of the car at my disposal. At the end of my training, I was assigned to Jay Engineering works (manufacturers of Usha fans and sewing machines) and found myself back in Calcutta at the corporate headquarters in a marketing role. I got my next big break when the company wanted someone willing to relocate to a subsidiary of Jay Engineering in Sri Lanka. Though it was primarily a commercial role, they required an Engineer to meet the visa criteria. I was selected for the job and within the 3rd year of my career, I was at the #3 position in the company. Suddenly, in my hands were all the business functions from sales & marketing, purchasing, HR, finance to corporate relations and this turned out to be a huge learning experience.

The Gifts of Crisis

After 2 years, the Sri Lankan government tightened visa norms for Indians working in subsidiary entities. We were 3 of us from India in the company and our visas were not renewed. While most perceived this as a crisis, it was a big favor for me from the Sri Lankan government because that brought me back to the bigger stage of my parent company. Otherwise, I would have drifted in that small entity for many years that would not have contributed to my growth as a manager. Once I was back in Calcutta, I embarked on a rapid growth path and began to handle much bigger responsibilities.

During the 1970s, the Naxalite movement was at its peak in Calcutta and violent attacks on policemen and working professionals was a common occurrence. One morning while I was on my way to the factory with my general manager and a couple of other colleagues, our car was attacked and my general manager and I sustained multiple injuries. We were rushed to the hospital and I had multiple stitches on my head. The next morning my parents read the news of this attack with photographs on the front page of the Hindustan Times.

My parents wanted me to quit my job and get out of Calcutta. But I didn't want to run away from the problem. I felt I had to be there and do my share of managing the company. This was not a reason to opt out. Since elections were due in 6 months and violence was expected to erupt any time, my parents wanted me to at least take a 2-week vacation during elections. I agreed.

During this vacation, I visited my sister in Bombay. I happened to see an ad in the newspaper, of an MBA program in the Asian Institute of Management in the Philippines. Although, I couldn't fulfill some of the criterion mentioned in the ad I went to the office of the representative (Dr. Jagdish Parikh) and told him that I had been planning to do an MBA but couldn't afford to do it in America. I had saved enough money for Philippines, thanks to my stint in Sri Lanka. The gentleman spent 15 minutes talking to me and said that I was the kind of candidate they would want and that I should apply. I got admission, took study leave to complete my MBA, came back to the same company, and became the GM of the Calcutta factory after a stint in Delhi. Every crisis is a blessing in disguise. Had it not been for the attack, I would not have taken the vacation to Bombay and would not have done my MBA, which helped to take my career to the next level.

At the age of 32, I became the general manager for Usha Fans factory in Calcutta, then, the largest fan factory in the world. I was given additional responsibility for Fan exports. We won every award in the industry during those 2 years. We won the State Award and National Award for fan exports. One day, my chairman, Lala Chatram called me to Delhi and said, 'Shriram Refrigeration, a group company is in grave danger. It will be the first company in our entire group to go bankrupt because we have been losing money for the last 5 years. At present it is reeling under a negative net worth. I want you to report next week and take charge of things because it's a crisis situation. I landed there in 1978 at the age of 34 as the CEO of the company. It's a wonderful feeling for me now; I have spent more than half my life as a CEO. It was a great opportunity. We turned the company around within 1 year retaining the same team. I sacked only 1 person. Though he was highly rated in his work, he was cynical about the turnaround effort and was a dent to the morale of the employees. The team got the message that it was everyone's role to positively contribute to the company's turnaround.

After the turnaround, the company grew rapidly, profits increased year over year and things became routine. I told my chairman that I wanted to do a Ph. D and that I wanted a 1- year-sabbatical to get it started. He was anxious about it initially but he agreed for 8 months. Therefore, I registered in Osmania University and then a strange thing happened. Suddenly Osmania University went on strike. I had negotiated my leave with so much difficulty and didn't want to forego the same. I decided to go to the USA for 3 to 4 months. I wove the trip around old college friends with whom I stayed.

This included Anand Khokha. By coincidence, a year later Azim Premji was in America and happened to meet Anand and asked him if he knew anyone who could run an IT company in India. So Anand referred my name. This was another great gift born out of crisis because if I hadn't met Anand after 19 years of college, he wouldn't have referred me and if I hadn't taken that vacation to the US, I wouldn't have met Anand and if Osmania University hadn't gone on strike, I wouldn't have taken that vacation. So I strongly believe that every problem, situation or challenge presents a new opportunity.

The Happy Days at Wipro

Azim Premji came back and got in touch with me. I was least interested. I told him, 'I have been working with this group for 19 years; I am running the business; why on earth would I want to join Wipro? I haven't even heard of Wipro before.' A little while later, Anand was in Bangalore. I was in Hyderabad and I decided to spend a day with him in Bangalore. In a discussion with Anand, Premji got to know that I was visiting Anand in Bangalore. He called me up and asked me to meet him in Bangalore and I agreed.

He spent half a day with me. I told him I had to leave for work. He said, 'Why don't you send me your resume?' I said, 'I don't have a resume and don't have the time to prepare one since it's the fag end of the financial year. I will send it to you after a couple of months.' Within a couple of weeks, Premji called me again and said, 'Forget the resume. Just come and meet me on a Sunday morning at my residence. I love Mr. Premji's style of getting in-depth. We started the meeting at 9 am. By lunchtime, I was ready to leave. He asked me to have lunch at his place and then the conversation continued till evening tea and then drinks. He asked me to stay for dinner as well but I said I had to leave because I was staying with a friend.

After that meeting, I got the offer and accepted it. At the age of 41, in May 1984, I ended up as the President of Wipro Infotech.

Between 1984 and 1991, Wipro Infotech shot past all other computer companies. In 1991, Mr. Premji offered me the position of CEO of Wipro Systems, which was then a struggling software business. I led the growth of Wipro's IT business from $2 million to $500 million run-rate and led it to become India's second largest software company (after TCS).

Leaving Wipro was inevitable for me. I had done an introspective exercise from a book on spiritual exercises (Wellsprings by Anthony D' Mello) during a vacation in Lakshadweep. One section of the book talks about one's unfulfilled desires. And I had two, one was to become an entrepreneur and the second was to write a book, which I have still not done. Two years before I finally quit, I actually did resign but Mr. Premji persuaded me to stay. Mr. Premji actually did a big favor by asking me to stay. During those two years that I stayed on, due to the dotcom boom, the stock prices and company valuations skyrocketed. If I had left 2 years earlier, we (Wipro) would have got $2 million and given away 51% of the company to the VCs. Now, we got $9.5million for which we gave away only 26% of the company to the VCs. That was a huge difference. The market was so hot that I got the commitment for the money through a phone call to the USA within half an hour of my leaving Premji's office.

The Happier Days at Mindtree

In 1999, I started Mindtree. Change has always represented opportunity, and at that time change was the Internet. Mindtree became an E-Systems integrator. Though one can say that I rode the wave of growth, but the truth is that I rode it much better than others.

Mindtree was an 8-month-old E-Systems integrator when the dotcom bubble burst. 99 out of 100 companies that started globally at that time collapsed, including many in the US. Mindtree survived because we re-strategized rapidly, introduced several new offerings and also because we had conserved our cash and could stay afloat till markets revived. The market revival in 2002 was followed by 5 years of 60% compounded growth. The culmination for me as the Founding Chairman & Managing Director of MindTree was to lead it through a very successful IPO in 2007.

The Happiest Days

At age 68, I chose to leave Mindtree and started another company. The reasons are very deeply personal. Many of my co-founders were persons who began their career with me and most acknowledged that Mind Tree would not have been around but for my leadership and decisions I took during the early, difficult years. And then a saddening event occurred. It took me only a few minutes to decide I could not work with them anymore, as things could never be the same again. In retrospect, I feel they did me a big favor because all crises or problems have always luckily turned out to be a blessing in disguise for me. I was 68 years. Logically at

70 I would have stepped aside to make way for the next person. However, given the sort of person I am, I feel young because I am engaged actively.

The event that motivated me to make a change opened up a brand new runway for me. I am thoroughly enjoying the new run. I have a great team and it has given me an opportunity to focus on a theme I was dwelling upon for a long time -- Happiness. Apart from all the strategic business opportunities, I am excited on how we can create a company whose mission is as simple as it could be – "Happiest People. Happiest Customers".

Happiest Minds Technologies is now in its 4th year and has a sharp focus on enabling Digital Transformation for customers by delivering a Smart, Secure and Connected experience through disruptive technologies like mobility, big data analytics, security, cloud computing, social computing, M2M/IoT, unified communications, etc. Enterprises are embracing these technologies to implement omni-channel strategies, manage structured and unstructured data and make real- time decisions based on actionable insights, while ensuring security for data and infrastructure. Happiest Minds also offers a high degree of skills, IPs and domain expertise across a set of focused areas that include Digital Transformation & Enterprise Solutions, Product Engineering Services, Infrastructure Management, Security, Testing and Consulting.

While I believe that Happiest Minds is still a success story in the making, at the end of its 3rd full financial year, Happiest Minds Technologies has built a team of 1,500 persons, achieved a run rate of $50 million and has 100 wonderful customers. All these are record levels for any company in the Indian IT Services industry in 3 years. Clearly the message of Happiness is resonating with customers and employees.

Learning from the Legend

So what makes me happy? And happiness as I define it, is a very personal, deep state of mind that is also at peace with itself. So every assignment I chose was based on fundamental beliefs.

1. Fulfilling my own potential, while helping others to fulfill their own;
2. Living my life true to myself rather than based on the expectations of others;
3. I have choices, including the choice to choose happiness.

You make your own luck, when you rely on your values, capabilities and performance. Right from the start of my career, I made decisions that may not have seemed easy or great in the short run but I know, they made a huge difference in the long run. Direction matters. Get the direction right and then reaching the destination is inevitable.

Ashok Soota

Ashok Soota, Executive Chairman, Happiest Minds, a next generation IT Services company, is widely recognized as one of the pioneering leaders of the Indian IT industry.

Prior to founding Happiest Minds in August 2011, Ashok led the growth of Wipro's IT business from $ 2m to$ 500m run-rate. Subsequently, he was founding Chairman & MD of MindTree and led it through a very successful IPO. His second entrepreneurial venture, Happiest Minds has already established several benchmarks in the IT Services industry in India and is on course to achieve its goal of being the fastest to achieve USD 100 Million revenue.

Ashok began his career in 1965 with the Shriram Group of Industries in India. In 1978, he became CEO of Shriram Refrigeration, a company which was unprofitable for four straight years. Ashok facilitated a complete turnaround, making it profitable in his very first year and taking it to a position of leadership in each of its product line.

Ashok is a leader of industry. He was President of Confederation of Indian Industry (CII), India's largest Industry association and also President of Manufacturers' Association of Information Technology. He has served on Prime Minister's Task Force for IT and on the Advisory Council for the World Intellectual Property Organization, Geneva. For his contributions to India's IT industry, he has been recognized twice as IT Man of the Year, also as Electronics Man of the Year, and recognized at Infocom 2013, Kolkata as one of the 12 Gems who helped to build Indian IT Industry. The companies he has led have created about 25,000 jobs during his leadership tenure. He is a recipient of the Prof S N Mitra Award from Indian National Academy of Engineering INAE), the Golden Peacock Award for Technology Leadership and the Most Innovative People

Award for Knowledge Innovation at the World Summit on Innovation and Entrepreneurship 2008. He has been a member of the Global Board of Trustees of TiE. He has served on the Board of Governors of IIM, Kozhikode and was the founding Chief Patron of Samarthanam Trust for the Disabled.

Ashok's philanthropic contributions are channeled through Ashirvadam, a Trust he has created for Environmental protection and help for the needy including vocational training, education and medical assistance.

Ashok holds a Bachelor of Engineering degree from Roorkee University (now IIT, Roorkee) and an MBA from the Asian Institute of Management, Philippines. He is a Fellow INAE. Ashok's hobbies include trekking, the outdoors, yoga, taichi, meditation and swimming.

ABOUT THE AUTHORS

This is a book written by industry experts, each contributing a chapter. Here's a list of all the CO-AUTHORS of this publication (in no particular order):

Rohit Bagaria
Rajesh Dembla
Parmeet Singh
Vivek Agarwal
Thumbay Moideen
Monika Singh

Sadananda Murthy
Ashok Soota
Avinash Sisode
Bhakti Sanghavi
Dr. Sunil Kumar

www.ingramcontent.com/pod-product-compliance
Lightning Source LLC
Chambersburg PA
CBHW070027210526
45170CB00012B/272